Zen Buddhism and Advaita Vedanta

A Comparative Study of History, Philosophy, and Practice

Zen Buddhism and Advaita Vedanta

A Comparative Study of History, Philosophy, and Practice

Dr. Varish Panigrahi
and
Debi Prasad Dash

BLACK EAGLE BOOKS
Dublin, USA | Bhubaneswar, India

 Black Eagle Books
USA address:
7464 Wisdom Lane
Dublin, OH 43016

India address:
E/312, Trident Galaxy, Kalinga Nagar,
Bhubaneswar-751003, Odisha, India

E-mail: info@blackeaglebooks.org
Website: www.blackeaglebooks.org

First International Edition Published by
Black Eagle Books, 2024

ZEN BUDDHISM AND ADVAITA VEDANTA
by **Dr. Varish Panigrahi** and **Debi Prasad Dash**

Copyright © Dr. Varish Panigrahi and Debi Prasad Dash

All rights reserved. No part of this publication may be reproduced, stored in a retrieval system, or transmitted, in any form or by any means, electronic, mechanical, photocopying, recording or otherwise without the prior permission of the publisher.

Cover & Interior Design: Ezy's Publication

ISBN- 978-1-64560-553-9 (Paperback)
Library of Congress Control Number: 2024938693

Printed in the United States of America

Preface

Zen belongs to the Mahayana sect of Buddhism and had a significant influence on East Asian countries, particularly China, Japan, Vietnam, and Korea. Zen germinated on the Mahayana ideals somewhere in the 4th-5th century CE in India and later spread to China through traveling monks in the 6th century CE. The Indian mystic Bodhidharma is credited with introducing Zen in China. Zen spread to the American and European countries in the twentieth century, after the Second World War. In the words of Professor Alan Watts, Zen may be regarded as the fruition of Indian, Chinese, and Japanese cultures and one of the precious gifts of Asia to the world.

On the other hand, Advaita Vedanta is a prominent sect of Hinduism based on Upanishadic philosophy which was compiled over hundreds of years before the Common Era. Adi Shankaracharya is considered to be the principal architect of the sect, founding it in the 8th century CE. However, his philosophy is an extension of his guru Goudapada's philosophy which in a way was Shankaracharya's homage to his prime teacher. He did an extensive study of the Vedas, Upanishads, and the Brahma Sutra that resulted in the formation of Advaita philosophy.

This book offers a comprehensive comparative analysis of the two non-dual philosophic sects of Buddhism and Hinduism. This book was developed as part of a research project at Kalinga ZEN Advaita Mahasangha operating under Kalinga ZEN Foundation Trust.

Since the inception of Kalinga ZEN Advaita Mahasangha, there has been an attempt to ambulate the best of Zen Buddhism and Advaita Vedanta as appropriate and dictated by the needs of its participants and members. The senior author of this book had attended the services at Ramakrishna Mission Center in Boston for almost two decades in the eighties and the nineties. He participated in half a dozen Zen retreats in the United States before the pandemic year 2020. So, there was a strong foundation of practice and philosophy from both traditions.

The first chapter is an introduction to Zen Buddhism and Advaita Vedanta. We have summarized some of the key points of both traditions so that the reader has an overall perspective as the following chapters delve deep into the topic.

The second chapter informs about the historical sojourn of Zen Buddhism and Advaita Vedanta as of the present date. The third, fourth, fifth, and sixth chapters comprise the body of this book and inform about the core philosophy of both traditions. It caters to Metaphysics, Epistemology, Ethics, and Aesthetics.

The seventh chapter is on the monastic and worldly lives of the Zen and Advaita practitioners and tries to illustrate the modern-day practice of these two traditions both in Asia and the West. The practice followed at Kalinga ZEN Advaita Mahasangha is based on the synthesis of both traditions.

The final chapter is the conclusion which has inputs from the authors from their own experience and study.

We hope that people in India and abroad read this book to get introduced to both Zen Buddhism and Advaita Vedanta since this book is written with the sole motive of giving a brief overview of both Zen Buddhism and Advaita Vedanta by studying and comparing them together. After reading this book, one may further delve deep into these traditions, for which this book serves as a good introduction.

We thank all members of the Kalinga ZEN Advaita Mahasangha for their encouragement during the preparation of this book. We specially thank Sashibhushan Rath for his comments and suggestions after reading the manuscript. We very much appreciate the prompt attention given by Ashok Parida and Satya Pattanaik of 'Black Eagle Books' Publications to the production of this book.

Finally, we thank Kalinga ZEN Foundation and its key sponsors Brig. Niranjan Dhal and Anuradha Panigrahi for their financial support, which led to the publication of this book.

CONTENTS

Chapter 1	Introductory Remarks	11
Chapter 2	Origin and History	19
	2.1 Introduction	21
	2.2 History of Zen Buddhism	22
	2.3 History of Advaita Vedanta	28
	2.4 Comparative Analysis	36
	References	37
Chapter 3	Metaphysics	39
	3.1 Introduction	41
	3.2 Metaphysics in Zen Buddhism	43
	3.3 Metaphysics in Advaita Vedanta	56
	3.4 Comparative Analysis	71
	References	79
Chapter 4	Epistemology	83
	4.1 Introduction	85
	4.2 Epistemology in Zen Buddhism	87
	4.2.1 Pratyaksha	88
	4.2.2 Anumana	91
	4.3 Epistemology in Advaita Vedanta	97
	4.3.1 Pratyaksha	98
	4.3.2 Anumana	101
	4.3.3 Upamana	103
	4.3.4 Shabda	105
	4.3.5 Arthapatti	108
	4.3.6 Anupalabdhi	112
	4.4 Comparative Analysis	117
	References	125

Chapter 5	Ethics and Morality	129
	5.0 Introduction	131
	5.1 Ethics in Zen Buddhism	131
	5.2 Ethics in Advaita Vedanta	144
	5.3 Comparative Analysis	155
	References	159
Chapter 6.0	Aesthetics	161
	6.0 Introduction	163
	6.1 Aesthetics in Zen Buddhism	166
	6.2 Aesthetics in Advaita Vedanta	173
	6.3 Comparative Analysis	180
	References	185
Chapter 7	Practice	189
	7.0 Introduction	191
	7.1 Practice in Zen Buddhism	192
	7.1.1 Institutions	192
	7.1.2 Scriptures	197
	7.1.3 Liturgy	206
	7.1.4 Koans	211
	7.1.5 Meditation	213
	7.2 Practice in Advaita Vedanta	216
	7.2.1 Institutions	217
	7.2.2 Scriptures	218
	7.2.3 Liturgy	220
	7.2.4 Stories and Enquiries	224
	7.2.5 Meditation	224
	7.3 Comparative Analysis	225
	References	226
Chapter 8	Concluding Remarks	231

Chapter 1

Introductory Remarks

Man is uniquely positioned as the bearer of reason and intellect. Wondering through the realms of philosophy, man's relentless pursuit of wisdom and understanding has unraveled many natural laws and secrets of the universe. There is so much man knows now about himself and the world he lives in. But his advancement has also made him aware of how much he does not know. So, man has not only made strides with his technological advancements but has also gathered more unanswered questions than ever. This has made him more self-aware about the necessity to satiate his spiritual urge.

In India, philosophy is intertwined with religion, and spirituality is often seen as the sweet result of such a consummation. It encompasses a wide range of philosophical thoughts offering a direct perspective on metaphysical, epistemological, and ethical qualms through deeply connected spiritual and aesthetic practices. But more so than just being highly explanatory and elaborative, Indian philosophy also offers a direct realization of the truth. It questions, if there is an absolute, and provides a reason for or against its certainty. Indian philosophy also gives a clear exposition on the status of the individual 'self', and its relationship with a primary creator. Indian philosophy is highly autonomous, and the differences in thoughts of different schools, sects, and traditions are not seen as alien or external to each other, but different ways to reach the same truth.

Buddhism, Hinduism, and Jainism are three such old traditions that bear the flagship of Indian spirituality and philosophy. Over time, these traditions evolved into major religions of the twenty-first century, with Hinduism and Buddhism being placed as the third and fourth largest religions in the world in terms of their following. Throughout recorded history, Hinduism has developed mostly in and around the Indian subcontinent but Buddhism spread to other countries adapting to local situations and simultaneously influencing its surroundings, particularly in China where Buddhism was brought as a version of Indian idealism. However, China had a rich philosophy of its own, particularly in Confucianism and Taoism. It was after this interaction, that a Chinese version of realism developed which was formalized as Chan. Subsequently, it spread to other countries like Japan, Vietnam, and Korea. It was in Japan, where the current name in use 'Zen' was assigned. Today Zen is understood as a school of Mahayana Buddhism that emphasizes on direct experience of enlightenment through meditation and intuition. Its philosophy advocates simplicity and minimalism. In the West, it is seen as a way to attain mindfulness and awareness. But Zen, according to D.T. Suzuki, is a way to know one's true self, and to do so, not as a final achievement or goal, but as the starting point of a unified, interconnected, and interdependent understanding of the world and its inhabitants.

Around the same time, as Chan was being developed in China, Hinduism was entering into a reformation, when the Upanishads took precedence over the Vedas, and spirituality was stated to be seen as an internal and introspective journey, rather than as external worship and a means to acquire heavenly gratification. Adi Shankaracharya was the frontrunner of this reformation and formalized an ancient philosophy of Advaita by infusing it into Vedanta, the essence of which is the ideation of a non-participating, all-pervading absolute in Brahman. Vedanta as the name suggests in Sanskrit, means the end of the Vedas. It also means the essence of the Vedas, which are the Upanishads.

By doing an extensive study of the Upanishads (Sruti) and certain selective Smriti, combined with his own experience, Shankaracharya declared that absolute reality is Advaita or nondual. And that the sole aim of the spiritual journey is to realize this truth and experience this reality.

This non-duality cannot be objectively confirmed, because the evidence of a dualistic, mind-dependent world is overburdening. This dualistic experience or false understanding of reality is the result of a deceptive power or an illusory veil called Maya that conceals the true nature of reality and in its place, projects a mind-constructed, temporarily placed, and appearance-based reality. It means what we see, only appears to be true, and is temporary. It is because of this deception, that there is a false appreciation for the self, or the urge to create an individual identity. Since nothing is set to last forever, one needs only to wake up from this slumber. And Advaita Vedanta offers a way, to come out of this illusion, to understand the real nature of the self, and to eventually realize its relationship with the absolute, all while developing a holistic nature within, where all is seen as the one, and one is seen in all.

Zen Buddhism, although rooted in the rich tradition of Mahayana Buddhism, offers a unique approach to spirituality and the awakening within. In many ways, Zen Buddhism is similar to Advaita Vedanta, particularly the idea, that what we see as real, is conditioned and only relative. And the truth is veiled from us, which is indeed the ultimate reality. Besides, both traditions are similar in declaring that the ultimate reality is non-dual. The subject of this book is the understanding of nonduality through the lens of Zen Buddhism and Advaita Vedanta. Both traditions are aligned in their advocacy for a non-dual-based reality, which is hidden from us because of our conditioning and inability to see through. But they vary in their understanding of such a reality and the way to achieve it. Zen Buddhism follows from the traditional Buddhist understanding of a nonduality-based reality, but does not affirm an absolute in place of it, and declares that reality is conditioned and dependent on moments. Each moment bears the potential of revealing the truth if one can only cultivate the necessary awareness or mindfulness to see the momentariness through each moment.

On the other hand, Advaita Vedanta also advocates for a non-dual reality in Brahman, which is without attribute, unconditioned, and permanent. The recognition of non-duality is considered essential for Moksha, and the essence of this understanding is encapsulated in the expression 'Tat Tvam Asi' or 'That Thou Art'. The profound philosophy of Advaita Vedanta and Zen Buddhism encourages to go beyond and tear through the surface level perceptions and intellectual understanding to directly experience the non-dual nature of reality.

The following chapters in this book delve deep into the philosophical underpinnings, analyze them separately under different headings and subheadings, and finally compare and contrast the findings individually. The chapters have been divided such that they cater to all aspects of philosophy, namely, history, metaphysics, epistemology, ethics, aesthetics, and practice, discussing in-depth, their scope and influence on both Zen Buddhism and Advaita Vedanta. The final chapter is an overall comparative analysis of the preceding chapters about both traditions. This book will provide its readers with a crucial understanding of the philosophical foundations of Zen Buddhism and Advaita

Vedanta, and a critical examination based on their shared similarities and differences. The book will also provide its readers, with ample evidence for shared practices, despite different settings in each tradition.

Overall, the book will encourage contemplation and inter-faith dialogue and discussion following a nuanced understanding of these Eastern philosophical traditions that flourished in India, China, and Japan more than a thousand years ago. To individuals seeking spiritual guidance, the book may be used in the beginner's spirit. This book does not claim to find anything new, which has already not been known about each tradition. Both traditions developed against specific backdrop, Zen Buddhism in China and Japan and Advaita Vedanta in India. Yet for all the differences that both traditions have against each other, which seems so prominent at the surface level, they offer subtle similarities, which beyond the surface level tension, seem to dissolve all differences. The essence is not in the content of these two traditions but in their intent.

Both traditions emphasize on transcending the dualities and realizing the non-dual nature of reality. They have their interpretations of nonduality. But clearly expressing their intent, both traditions advocate for direct insight and experience of the self, insofar that all distinctions between the self and the other dissolve.

Finally, to the readers, the book should be used as a guide or an introduction to the contrasting yet similar philosophy of Zen Buddhism and Advaita Vedanta. The authors urge the readers of the book to engage in thoughtful reflection on the insights offered by both traditions. The authors further encourage their readers, to embrace the shared essence of both traditions, which is imbibed in transcendence, transmission, and transformation. A thoughtful call would be not to engage with the philosophy offered by both traditions as mere concepts or information but as pathways to an impersonal experience of an interconnected reality. The authors are hopeful, that the book serves as a bridge to cultural divides, and that its readers appreciate the rich and insightful philosophy offered by Zen Buddhism and Advaita Vedanta.

Chapter 2

Origin and History

2.1. Introduction

This chapter will explore the origin and the historical background of Zen Buddhism and Advaita Vedanta, the two non-dual schools of philosophy, each branching from a separate religion. Zen is based on the Mahayana School of Buddhism and started in India but fully developed later in China and Japan. Advaita Vedanta belongs to the Vedanta school of Hinduism and originated, developed, and evolved in India.

Mahayana Buddhism emerged around the beginning of the first century CE in India. Its philosophy spread throughout Asia as part of expansive Buddhism that flourished because of its broad views on enlightenment. The Mahayanists firmly believe that an enlightened person postpones his liberation to help other sentient beings reach Nirvana. When this altruistic idea reached China, it didn't find much resistance from the local philosophic schools of that time. In the sixth century CE, a separate Buddhist school developed called Chan, derived from the word *Dhyana*. It absorbed local cultures and beliefs, while maintaining its core Buddhist ideals, particularly the idea of pursuing enlightenment for the benefit of all beings. Gradually it spread to Japan where it was developed further and was called Zen. From Japan Zen spread to the rest of the world in the twentieth century. This chapter will briefly discuss the connection of India, China, and Japan in light of Zen Buddhism.

On the other hand, Advaita Vedanta is a Brahmanical school based on the Vedanta philosophy of Hinduism. Its genesis is attributed to Adi Shankaracharya of the 8th century CE, who revitalized and crystallized the ancient teachings of the Upanishads and the Brahma sutras. At its heart,

Advaita Vedanta is a non-dual school of Hindu philosophy, with its origin shrouded in mysticism. The philosophy of Advaita cannot be traced back to any particular founder, but there are great saints, scholars, and masters who have significantly contributed to the philosophy of Advaita Vedanta. Shankaracharya is the most celebrated preacher cum philosopher and is often credited as its founder. He never claimed any title, but because of his significant involvement in the codification of Advaita Vedanta, he is considered as its most important figure. This chapter will also discuss the history surrounding the revival movement that led to the rise of Hinduism and the decline in popularity of other subsequent religions, particularly Buddhism in India.

2.2. History of Zen Buddhism

The school of Zen meaning *Dhyana* or meditation, is different from the other schools of Buddhism because it does not rely solely on the outward presentation of meditative practice for the sake of doing it. As the name suggests, Zen is supposed to have developed as a specific meditation school of Buddhism in its country of birth, India. However, there are no historical traces left of the specific school in Buddhist India. All knowledge important in Zen is traditional knowledge passed down through the discipline of lineage and masters. However, the origins of Zen are shrouded in legends.

As the legend goes, the Buddha while once preaching to a large audience, was felicitated with flowers and gifts by the crowd. Among the things presented to him was a bouquet which he picked up without uttering a word. To the crowd, fixated on him, this was surprising, as they anxiously waited for the master to speak. This gesture had a meaning and as the Zen legend goes, only *Mahakasyapa* was able to decode the meaning of the gesture by the Buddha. This incident is supposedly the origin of the Zen doctrine of Buddhism that was passed on by 27 Zen masters until it was introduced to China many centuries later.

Zen scholars refer to 520 CE as the significant year of the Zen foundation when Bodhidharma, the South Indian Buddhist traveling from India arrived in China. He is called the first patriarch of Zen in China. A patriarch is the spiritual head of a lineage, who in Buddhism is the keeper and revealer of the formal transmission of Buddha's teachings. The responsibility of leading the Zen monks is transferred to the next patriarch by the previous one, administered through lines of succession within the sect. *Bodhidharma* came to China to teach a method of 'direct realization' different from all other schools of Buddhism already established in China. Although there are conflicting accounts regarding the origin of Zen, in the present context, Zen scholarship is unbothered regarding the historical situation of Zen. As D. T Suzuki says, whether the school started in India with the Buddha, or in China with *Bodhidharma*, the only connection that matters is the ideal and logical connection of the Mahayana philosophy of universal salvation and enlightenment and its thorough actualization in China and Japan.

The history and origin of Zen are speculative and suggestive, but the scriptural sutra foundations cannot be denied for Zen. Based upon the four Mahayana sutras, namely, *Prajnaparamita Hridaya Sutra, Vajracchedika Sutra, Lankavatara Sutra, and Saddharma Pundarika Sutra*, Zen Buddhism, evolved in China and subsequently flourished in Japan and all over Asia [1]. *Prajnaparamita Hridaya Sutra* or the Heart Sutra, discusses in detail the compassion of *Bodhisattvas*. It's in the form of a dialectic between the *Bodhisattva Avalokitasvara* and the chief disciple Shariputra, wherein the *Bodhisattva* reveals the details of his enlightened experience to the latter. The true understanding of *Prajna-Paramita Sutra* is the fact that in the absence of anything permanent, the only thing that remains is emptiness [2]. All sentient beings are a composite of the five *Skandhas* which are all empty. Emptiness implies that there is no innate essence or value to anything, and the phenomenal world is only a combination of different factors working together.

All things are just phenomena, created and working in the presence of other phenomena. Some things seem permanent, but relatively just, only to be replaced by subsequent things, thus confirming the changing nature of reality.

The *Vajracchedika Sutra* or the Diamond Sutra is a revered scripture in Zen teachings. It is in the form of a conversation between the Buddha and his disciple Subhuti regarding the experience of emptiness and momentary existence as to be the nature of reality. Besides, it also emphasizes the limitations of vernacular expression to explain the true nature of ultimate reality [3]. Such is its reverence among Zen practitioners, it is believed that Hui-Neng, the 6th Chinese patriarch, is supposed to have attained enlightenment (*Satori*), just by listening to the verses of the *sutra*.

It is believed that Hui-Ko, the second Chinese patriarch, received a copy of the translated manuscript from Bodhidharma. It discusses the participation of the mind in the construction of our reality as being a mere projection of consciousness [4]. Our consciousness being the storehouse of all our past experiences, reveals them by the law of karma in subsequent births. It also speaks of the *'Tathagatagarbha'*, or the innate Buddha nature being deeply seeded in every human being, thus making him capable of attaining liberation by cultivating the seed within. Owing to its complexity and unsystematic approach, the *Lankavatara Sutra* is not as popular today as it was before. Its study is primarily done under the guidance of experienced masters and referred to in the advanced stages of spiritualism.

Finally, the *Saddharma Pundarika Sutra,* or the Lotus Sutra is one of the earliest Sutras based on the teachings of the Buddha. He considered this sutra to be his most important one. It empowers ordinary human beings with the capability to cultivate 'sheer will' to achieve *Nirvana*. Common people can end their suffering through faith and devotion to Buddha. A person in flesh and blood transcends into the *Dharma* itself by way of devotion to the universal Buddha or *Dharmakaya* and attains *Nirvana* [5].

Many scholars, particularly D.T. Suzuki, argue that Bodhidharma only introduced a new method of meditation to the Chinese people. But it took more than two hundred years, for Zen to have fully evolved and its message being truly understood [6]. The true beginning of the Zen school, according to some scholars can be credited to the appointment of Hui-Neng as the 6th Chinese Zen patriarch.

Hui-Neng considered the goal of Zen practice was to find out one's 'self-nature'. And this according to D.T Suzuki, is the most significant understanding of Zen practice and meditation as such. The true practice of Zen is to reflect within and not to attain any physical or eternal reward. According to Hui-Neng, Zen is not about practicing meditation nor does it imply attaining liberation but it only asks to look within and find out the real self-nature [7]. Hui-Neng is celebrated by some scholars as the second founder of Zen Buddhism having transformed Zen as an evolved but Chinese form of Buddhism. As the story goes, he was neither an intellectual nor a scholar or a monk. He was a poor wood seller, who upon hearing the verses of *Vajracchedika Sutra*, became desirous of studying the sutra with a master of Buddhist doctrine. His ordinance into the Buddhist brotherhood and subsequent appointment as the 6th Zen patriarch is the confirmation of the new outlook that Mahayana Buddhism introduced to the world. It marked the great shift from the intellectualization and philosophizing in Buddhism to the simple- mindedness of locating the self, realizing the truth of non-duality and directness of practice and goal, through Zen Buddhism [8]. He insisted upon self introspection and advocated about the knowledge that comes from self-within. He was also famous for having pinned greater importance on willpower than on enlightenment. For enlightenment is not achieved either through high intellectualism or silent contemplation. It is done through the grasping of the mind and being aware of the self-nature.

The period from 6th to 9th CE is considered the golden age in Zen history [9]. This was the time when China was ruled by the T'ang dynasty. Hui-Neng, the 6th Chinese Zen patriarch, successfully reoriented the doctrine of Zen that remained the consensus authority among successive Zen schools and sects. Any differences among the followers were settled under the banner of Hui-Neng's teachings. Such was his grandeur that his followers spread across lands and started the 2nd important movement in the history of Zen, known as the 'Zen of the Patriarchs' [10]. The initial Zen values were founded upon the sacred teachings of the

Buddha that remained an exclusivity of Zen understanding. The masters referred to the sutra knowledge for teaching to their students. The original legend of the starting of the Zen traces back to the Buddha's enlightenment. But Hui-Neng's impact was such that, subsequent Zen followers, started crediting the patriarchs starting from Bodhidharma as the perfect transmitters of the Buddha's teachings. The Zen practitioners minimized their reliance on the claims of the sutras and were encouraged to witness the live testimony of the enlightened Zen patriarchs about their Buddha experience.

One such Zen master named Pai-Chang developed the Zen rule book for monastery life during this period. His contribution to the ethics and aesthetics of the Zen monastic life has enriched itself as a unique and different school of Mahayana Buddhism. Hei-Neng transformed Zen from a Buddhist export of Indian idealism to Chinese realism. Pai-Chang ensured that the uniqueness of the Zen movement is cemented along with all of Mahayana Buddhism. Its popularity grew and spread across nations because it presented a fresh perspective to the Buddha's message.

The next big development for Zen happened in the 12th CE when the Japanese Buddhist monk Myoan Eisai of the Tendai School traveled to China to learn about Zen principles, only to return and start a Zen sect in his native country, known as Rinzai Zen [11]. By the time Eisai traveled to China, all the major developments in the Zen technique were already in place and there was a consistency in its practice through a sincere commitment to lineage and adherence to Zen tradition. The other important sect of Japanese Zen, the Soto Zen School was founded by Master Eisai's pupil Ethei Dogen in the following years. There was a third Zen School started by another master Ingen in the 17th CE, but it gradually merged into the Rinzai sect.

In the 21st century, Zen Buddhism is practiced in Japan, China, Korea, and Vietnam among the Asian countries. Zen Buddhism is perhaps the best export of missionary Buddhism in the West as more and more Westerners are adopting Zen Buddhism. It can be argued that the idea of Zen sprouted in India, it was developed by the Chinese, but it was actualized in the lands of Japan, where it stands out to be the pre-eminent school of Buddhism today amongst all the Buddhist schools.

2.3. History of Advaita Vedanta

In the previous section, we traced the history of Zen Buddhism back to the initial ideas proposed by Mahayana Buddhism of India. Mahayana sutras were compiled and formalized by Ashwaghosha and later Nagarjuna. Mahayana sutras are the earliest texts known to Mahayana Buddhists and are known as Agamas believed to have been written around the start of the first century CE. Likewise, in the Advaita tradition, the Upanishads are considered the principal source of inspiration behind Badrayana's (5th century BCE) composition, called Brahmasutra, also known as Vedanta Sutras. And the Brahmasutra along with the Upanishads and Bhagavad Gita are the primary scriptures in the early development of Advaita philosophy. It is suggested that Gaudapada systematically propounded the ideas of *Ekapratijna*, the philosophy of one without the second, also known as Advaita Vedanta or the philosophy of non-dualism.

Gaudapada lived in the 5th century CE. His teachings were passed on to Govindapada and subsequently to Adi Shankaracharya, who further systematized Advaita

Vedanta and established the cornerstones of the Sanatana faith. His metaphysical theory of *Ajativada* (non-origination) is a critical explanation of the causational debate. Whether the world originates or not, from a single unit to many modifications, it is an irrelevant speculation, because whatever appears as real, is ultimately an illusion. Hence nothing gets created ever. There is an ultimate reality but without the assured plurality and diversity that is the world [12]. This understanding of the Jagat forms the inspiration for '*Maya*' which is the unleashed power of the Brahman without its participation, and 'apparent reality', which is the idea that reality is not untrue but only apparently just, but ultimately is an illusion. These two concepts are the cornerstone of understanding absolute reality through Advaita Vedanta.

Gaudapada was not the founder of Advaita Vedanta. Like many Indian traditional philosophies, the source of Advaita Vedanta is shrouded in mystery. The Advaita literature is an interpretation of the Vedas but through the Upanishads as its medium. So technically the early philosophy of Advaita Vedanta is based on the final understanding of the Upanishads. And like the Vedas, or the Upanishads, the origin of Advaita Vedanta, cannot be accredited to any particular founder. There are only great masters. There are some early mystic seers, who predate Shankaracharya or even Badryayana (composer of Vedanta Sutras), who might have contributed to the mystical evolution of the Advaita tradition [13]. Some of the mentioned names are of sages in Badryana's Brahmasutra, namely Asmarathya, Audulomi, and Kasakritsna. Not much is known about them except that they made practical translations and subjective interpretations of the Upanishads. Other names referred to by both of them in their works are Atreya, Bharattrprapanca, Karsnajini, Dravidacharya, Jaimini, Badari, and Tanka. Shankaracharya refers to certain Vrttikara in his works, who were early commentators on Brahmasutra. One such sage's name he mentions in his works is Upavasra [14], the author of Sarirakamimamsa-Vrtti, the earliest known commentary on Brahmasutra. Also mentioned above is Atreya, who was a sage in Mahabharata practicing non-duality.

Some scholars argue that Yajnavalka (7th Century BCE) who predates all others, should be credited as the first expounder of Advaita Vedanta [15] since he is considered to be the first to interpret the Brahman identity as both the immanent Ishvara and the transcendental reality. Yet for all the evidence for the world, these are but two parts of the same supreme reality, which is essentially nondual, and is unaffected by the apparentness of reality that tends to veil that nature through modifications and plurality. But most scholars agree that Adi Shankaracharya in the 7th century CE, gave a thorough rendition of Advaita's understanding based on the scriptural authority of the Upanishads, testimonial evidence of masters before him, and his own spiritual experience. It is suggested that it was Gaudapada, however, who inspired Shankaracharya to further develop and solidify the foundations for Advaita Vedanta. Besides being influenced by the Upanishads, the Brahmasutras, and the Bhagavad Gita, Gaudapada, also drew inspiration from Mahayana Buddhism, especially from Nagarjuna's *Sunyavada* and Vasubandhu's *Vijnanavada* [16]. This helped him compose his magnum opus, the Mandukya Karika, also known as the Gaudapada Karika, which according to modern scholars, is the first organized exposition on Advaita Vedantic philosophy.

The problem with this narrative is that to scholars like K.C. Bhattacharya, Gaudapada's Buddhist influence is a confirmation of the accusation that he was a Buddhist in disguise. But the viewpoint, that is also the gist of this book is the suggestion that both Mahayana Buddhism and Advaita Vedanta are not opposed philosophies, but rather two assured ways of spiritual development having had originally based on the teachings of the Upanishads, just like the two sides of the same coin. Many Upanishads, like the Brhadaranyaka and Chandogya Upanishads, predate Buddhism. Some Upanishads, like the Aitareya, Taittiriya, Kathaka, Mundaka, etc. were composed after the advent of Buddhism and in them, there is evidence of Buddhist inspiration.

Taking the baton from Gaudapada, Adi Shankaracharya expanded on the philosophy of Advaita Vedanta and stood as a stalwart spreading the philosophy of Advaita Vedanta and simultaneously defending the status of Sanatana Dharma or Hindu religion which was challenged by the rise of Buddhism in India. Historically, Shankaracharya is believed to have lived in the 8th and 9th century AD. During such times, he developed a philosophic temper at a very early age. He acquired the knowledge of the scriptures more than any other of his contemporizes of that time at a very tender age and applied that wisdom to reinterpret Brahmanism as Vedanta as it was the need of the hour [17]. He used the teachings of Advaita Vedanta, as a medium to reestablish the authority of the Vedas and segregate ten principal Upanishads from the lot.

His actions, marked a great shift, from the external ritualistic worshiping of the Brahman, to the internal, subjective introspection and subsequent self-identification with Brahman. In Shankara's own words, Vedanta segregates itself from other schools of philosophies at that time in the sense that, while other schools work towards an empirical determination of the 'objective truth of all things', Vedanta works towards a revealed understanding wherein the objective truth is forsaken for a 'subjective identification in all things' [18]. That, there is a hidden truth beneath the surface and it can be revealed is the overall proposition of Advaita Vedanta. Up and above the surface is a deceit full of appearances that seem real, insofar as the events of a dream do. But like the dream vanishes, when one wakes up from his slumber, the veiled illusion of an objective reality unravels into a tranquil and permanent state of absoluteness, when one understands the true nature of reality.

Chief among Shankaracharya's disciples were Suresvara, Mandana Misra, Vacaspati Misra, and Padmapada. They along with Padmapada's disciples Prakasatman and Anandagiri, elaborated on the philosophy of Shankaracharya's Advaita Vedanta through their iterations. All of them have at some point been directly taught by Shankaracharya. The time from 7th to 9th century CE could be called the golden age of Advaita Vedanta. As evidence suggests, Shankaracharya along with his disciples, some of whom were his contemporaries whom he defeated into submission, have developed the age-old tradition of Advaita Vedanta into an unparalleled interpretation of Upanishads based on doctrines of 'absolutism' and 'non-duality'. The fundamentals in Shankara's metaphysics are based on the union of the self with the one (*Atmaiktva*) [19]. This union is not bound to its observable evidence, and reason alone is insufficient for the union to happen. Reason only is applicable insofar as it is used to understand the scriptural authority. But at some point, a transition must happen based on intuitive experience, where authority is shifted to spiritual experience and it is subjective. So, the union of the self in true terms means the 'I' identification where the I is not identified as something intelligible but intelligence itself, not as someone becoming but the very being itself and not in some form of ecstasy but in eternal peace.

Suresvara lived at the same time as Shankara and has made significant contributions to the theories of *'Maya'*, as an Advaita fundamental. He refers to *Maya* as a gate through which Brahman enters into many fold manifestations. Brahman is both the cause and effect of *Maya*. Mandana Misra lived around the same time as Suresvara or might have come after him, but he was also a direct disciple of Shankara. He is said to have abandoned his previous tradition in favor of the one started by Shankaracharya following a defeat by the latter in a debate based on knowledge and understanding of the scriptures. As a disciple of Kumarila Bhatta, he was an accomplished proponent of Mimamsa [20]. As a follower of Advaita, he composed the Brahma Siddhi, one of the foundational literature in Advaita Vedanta.

Mandana Misra did not contribute more to Advaita literature apart from his work on Brahma Siddhi but was instrumental in teaching Vacaspati Misra, who founded the first sub-school of Advaita Vedanta called Bhamati. According to some scholars, Vacaspati Misra belonged to one generation after Shankara. His commentaries on the works of Shankara and Mandana Misra are perhaps the most important literature in Advaita's understanding after Shankara's. Through his works, he assigned individual status to *Avidiya* [21], for there are any number of *Avidiya* as the number of individuals. He understands the individual self as the product of *Ajnana* (ignorance).

Opposing the Bhamati ideas of Vacaspati Misra, Padmapada, another direct disciple of Shankara, founded the Vivarana school of Advaita Vedanta. His legacy was forwarded by his disciple Prakasatman who lived in 12th-13th CE. The Vivarana School is often credited to the student disciple duo of Padmapada and Prakasatman. His theory of *Mulavidya* theorizes that *Maya* should be seen as a positive force of Brahman [22]. Although Brahman is the essential substance in all things and this is confirmed through the activity of *Maya* through which Brahman expresses itself. Another important metaphysical development in Advaita Vedanta happened during this time. Objective reality and its knowledge appear to be real but momentary just, and experience of it cannot be denied as false even if it is ultimately proven as mere illusion.

Following Shankara and his disciples, Advaita Vedanta established itself as the first systematic interpretation of Upanishadic teaching in general and Vedantic understanding in particular, while staying true to the Vedic heritage of Sanatana Dharma. The popularity of Advaita Vedanta and its most accomplished master Shankara, inspired philosophers like Ramanujacharya and Madhva, who gave their interpretation of Vedanta and Brahman, and subsequently established separate schools of Vedanta. Almost in all schools of Vedanta, the adherence to tradition (*Sampradaya*) is paramount. Shankaracharya was instrumental in popularizing the 'absolutist' understanding of Brahman, which he subsequently used to establish the non-negotiable authority of the selected scriptures. Primary among these are the principal Upanishads, Brahmasutras, and Bhagavad Gita, collectively known as Prasthanatryi. He also was supposed to have started monasticism for Advaita practitioners. Since then, the monastic life in the journey of an Advaita practitioner is considered necessarily important.

By the end of the 9th century CE, Advaita Vedanta had established itself as a dominant tradition and is often credited as being an instrumental movement in the saving of the Hindu religion. Its metaphysical foundations were unshakable, and its philosophy unrivaled. Some scholars like Radhakrishnan think that the rise of Advaita Vedanta contributed to the decline and substantial migration of Buddhism to other countries. However, throughout this time, many Advaita masters contributed to Advaita literature through original works on epistemology and commentaries on metaphysics. In the 17th CE, Dharmarajadvairindra, an important Advaita master composed Vedanta Paribhasa, which serves as an excellent rendition of logic and epistemology. This period is important in the history of Advaita Vedanta because he developed the Advaita theory of knowledge and treated epistemology and metaphysics separately.

Scholars argue that Mahayana Buddhism has more similarities with Advaita Vedanta than with any other Hindu school of thought. The evidence is obvious since both the tradition's background is based on the Upanishads. Advaita Vedanta draws its inspiration from the Brahmanism of Upanishads, phenomenalism of Buddhism, and other dharmic schools of that time, yet is a fresh perspective that never compromised itself as repetitive of some philosophy or derivative of any school. It stood the test of time and is truly the first true school of monistic idealism that advocated for a non-dual absolute.

2.4 Comparative Analysis

Zen Buddhism and Advaita Vedanta are distinct traditions with rich philosophy and spiritual content having played significant roles in their local settings when it mattered. Zen Buddhism has developed the most in China and Japan. Though considered a form of Mahayana Buddhism that traveled to China from India, it introduces itself as a new way of studying the doctrine of enlightenment through meditation, and not based on the mere philosophy of the scriptures. Zen is largely responsible for popularizing Mahayana Buddhism and its innovative and adaptive style of spiritualism in the West.

On the contrary, Advaita Vedanta was entirely developed and evolved within India and historically, played a significant role in the reviving of Hinduism when it faced stiff competition from the rise of Buddhism and the increased popularity of other forms of Hinduism like Shaktism, Vaishnavism, and Shaivism. Its roots can be traced back to the Upanishads, which are the ancient Indian texts, some of which date back to 800 BCE.

Both Zen Buddhism and Advaita Vedanta share a commitment to spiritual realization by perfecting the practice of meditation. In Zen, the practice of meditation is more prevalent and the entire activity of a Zen practitioner revolves around having a direct realization through meditation. Advaita Vedanta is more about reorienting the correct message of the Vedas through a reinterpretation of the Upanishads. Its most celebrated master, Adi Shankaracharya, was instrumental in marking a shift in the attitude of the Hindus, who before the popularization of

Advaita practiced, external worship and ritualistic sacrifices more as a way to earn themselves heavenly pleasures than connect with the divine. Shankara popularized the concept of 'man is divine', hence all introspection and scrutiny must be done to realize this divinity, of which man is unaware.

The core philosophy in both Advaita Vedanta and Zen Buddhism is about the realization of the sameness amidst the differences. This sameness or equilibrium according to Zen is called *'Sunyata'* and for Vedanta, it is *'Purnata'*. As history stood witness, both philosophic schools have been very influential in spreading their respective religions, and have stood the test of time for more than a thousand years. And today, it won't be wrong to say that both represent themselves as the most popular forms of Eastern philosophy in the West. Advaita Vedanta is the most accomplished form of Vedanta that there is. Similarly, Zen Buddhism is the most popular form of the Mahayana sect that has been hugely instrumental and successful in the spread of Buddhism.

References

1. *Zen Buddhism: Doctrinal Foundations and Practice, Varish Panigrahi, Page 58*
2. *Ibid Page-62-63*
3. *Ibid Page-71*
4. *Ibid Page-75,76,77*
5. *Ibid Page-73-74*
6. *Selected Writings of D, T Suzuki: Zen Buddhism, William Barrett, Page-87*

7. *Ibid Page-88*
8. *Ibid Page-86*
9. *Zen Buddhism: A History (India & China), Heinrich Dumoulin, Page-170*
10. *Ibid-Page-155-156*
11. *Zen Buddhism, Christmas Humphries, Page-37*
12. *Bhamati and Vivarana Schools of Advaita Vedanta, P.S. Roodurmum, Page-23*
13. *Ibid, Page-9*
14. *Ibid, Page-10*
15. *Ibid, Page-10*
16. *A Critical Survey of Indian Philosophy, D Sharma, Page-241*
17. *Indian Philosophy-Vol 2, S Radhakrishnan, Page-434*
18. *Bhamati and Vivarana Schools of Advaita Vedanta, P.S. Roodurmum, Page-27*
19. *Ibid, Page-27*
20. *Ibid, Page-31*
21. *Ibid, Page-36-37*
22. *Ibid, Page-41*

Chapter 3

Metaphysics

3.0 Introduction

Metaphysics is a branch of philosophy that explores the fundamental nature of existence and the underlying principles that govern reality. Its study is also concerned with investigating the conditions that define and shape our perception. It asks questions like whether individual experiences, are part of the external world or not. Its study is also pivotal to understanding the relationship between mind and matter. Such that it also asks, whether the mind is truly real, or the matter is real, or both are real? There is also a possibility that nothing is real, and all we see is an illusion or maybe we all are inside a simulation. Metaphysics demands that one seek information beyond surface-level observations and empirical data to understand much deeper and abstract aspects of reality, existence, and being.

Metaphysical investigation in Eastern philosophy offers a spectrum of perspectives, where individual philosophers are celebrated because they offer blends or modifications to complex metaphysical ideas, offering a nuanced viewpoint to understand reality. It is often characterized by its diversity rather than just adhering to one philosophical framework. Arguably, the study of metaphysics in Eastern philosophy is more intertwined with spirituality than its Western counterpart, which is more concerned about the development of philosophical thought through scientific inquiry. It is in that spirit that the current chapter will delve into the metaphysical foundations of Zen Buddhism and Advaita Vedanta.

Zen, a system deep-seated in the rich soil of Mahayana Buddhism, offers a unique perspective to the metaphysical landscape by transcending conventional understanding of it. The ancient tradition has its roots in India and can be traced back to the teachings of the Buddha. However, it was reborn in China and was subsequently developed in Japan. Bodhidharma, the Indian mystic, sowed the seeds of Chan (Zen) in the Chinese minds when he traveled to China in the 6th century CE. The word Zen is derived from Chan, which is the adaptation of the Sanskrit word Dhyana meaning meditation. Gradually, it developed into an elaborate system of its own, with a central focus on contemplative practices like meditation, and self-awareness.

On the other hand, Advaita Vedanta is a profound school of thought within the vast array of Indian philosophy, developed on the back of a strong objection to ordinary perception regarding the external world (Jagat) and the self (Atman). It is rooted, in the ancient scriptures called the Upanishads, and presents a radical understanding of reality by challenging the conventional assumptions regarding what is real, and how to know it. At its core, is the principle of non-duality (Advaita), which is an assertion that the external world, is an illusion. And that, one has to look through the illusion, to experience ultimate reality (Brahman or Advaita).

Metaphysical studies in Zen start with a caution to not fall into the entrapment by philosophical doctrines and scriptural testimonies. In Zen, the study of scriptures, doctrines, and testimonies is justified insofar as they serve a purpose. The purpose is to direct the mind towards focused meditation. Zen derives all its tenets from the Buddha's teachings, but it also declares that this knowledge if overburdened may become an obstacle to realization. Perhaps this is the same thing that Linji Yixuan, a prominent

Zen master of the 9th Century China said to his disciples, 'Kill the Buddha, when you see one'.

Metaphysics in Advaita Vedanta is an elaborate system comprising a three-way interlinking relationship between the external world (Jagat), the individual self (Atman), and the ultimate reality (Brahman). Once the relationship is understood, through accurate reading of the scriptures, the right interpretation of the masters, and application of true self-effort, one heeds for the final realization of the divine oneness of reality. Advaita Vedanta, which primarily credits the doctrinal ideas proposed by Sri Adi Shankaracharya, advocates for an intuitive understanding of reality over logic. Similarly, Zen which subscribes to Mahayana Buddhism also appeals for a direct understanding of reality. Both Zen Buddhism and Advaita Vedanta, explore the concept of an absolute reality, but they largely vary in their approach from the cultural, philosophical, and methodological perspectives.

3.1 Metaphysics in Zen Buddhism

Dr. D. T Suzuki says that Zen Buddhism is a way to realize the nature of one's true self [1]. This seems a very contradictory statement, given that Buddhism teaches Anatta or Anatman, which are the terms explaining the absence of a permanent and unchanging self. The Buddhists also do not believe in any final union with a creator [2]. There is no God and no soul in Buddhism. There is no essence at the basis of consciousness. And there is no fundamental reality that can be described or conceptually grasped. So, the 'true self' here, refers to a deeper understanding of the 'self' that goes beyond the ordinary understanding of it.

What is Zen?

Zen is the meditative sect of Buddhism and aims to attain the union of the body and the mind through deep meditation, to reach an enlightened stage. Understanding Zen metaphysics would be impossible if one is unfamiliar with Buddhist ways. The fundamental tenets of Buddhism are formed on the testimony of the Buddha's life itself, such that how he lived and what he taught covers Buddhism in its entirety.

One of the key concepts of Buddhism is Sunyata or the concept of emptiness. Unlike its literal meaning, Sunyata does not signify a void or absence, but rather in a unique way points to the interdependence and interconnectedness of all phenomena. This interconnectedness forms the basis of Zen metaphysics, challenging the dualistic framework that separates the self from the other. Zen rejects to see the world in terms of opposites and extremes and proposes to see everything as an essential interdependent sequence of events.

Zen teaches that ordinary understanding of reality is clouded by conceptual dualities and obsessive attachments. The mind conditioned by duality tends to perceive reality only through opposites and binaries, creating differences, and dividing the world into separate identities. This sense of separation and division, often locks perceptions into fixed categories, associating it with Nama and Rupa. This in turn prevents one from getting a holistic understanding of an interconnected reality. This interconnectedness caters to all aspects of reality. This means that no phenomenon exists in isolation, and everything is intimately connected and interwoven. It also transcends all artificial boundaries and assigned identities, referring to a dynamic interplay of relationships, affecting one another. Since all phenomena affect one another, Zen recognizes and acknowledges the diversity and multiplicity of the various facets of existence, but underlying is a unity that connects everything.

Influence of Madhyamika and Yogacara schools

Among the Mahayana schools, the Madhyamika philosophy of Nagarjuna and the no-mind doctrine of Yogacara have had a significant influence on the design of Zen metaphysics. The Madhyamika philosophy attributed to Nagarjuna talks about Sunyata or the absence of inherent existence emphasizing the interdependent and interconnected nature of all phenomena. Zen incorporated Nagarjuna's teachings with a strong emphasis on Sunyata. The concept is a deep insight into the understanding of reality without the idea of a substance or essence. Nagarjuna was a strong advocate of the Middle Way, which was a straightforward rejection of the extreme positions of absolutism and nihilism. Zen resonates with Nagarjuna's Middle Way, by avoiding any fixation on extreme views and emphasizing a non-dual realization.

The Yogacara School brought about the concept of 'reality as thought' [3]. In Buddhist nomenclature, the meaning of thought, mind, and consciousness are used interchangeably as the same meaning. The Yogacara School has had a significant influence on Zen Buddhism, in shaping doctrinal aspects.

Yogacara emphasizes the 'mind-only' or 'CittaMatra' philosophy, suggesting that all phenomena are generated by the mind and are merely mental constructs. So, the training of the mind is necessary to perceive reality beyond conceptual constructs and thinking.

The mind is both an obstruction and the key to a true awakening of consciousness. To do so, Zen proposes to reach an advanced state of no mind. The term 'no-mind' does not imply the absence of mental faculties, but refers to a more advanced state of consciousness characterized by the absence of regular thoughts and common chatter. It is a profound state of absolute mental stillness and clarity where the mind is not attached to its thoughts and constructs. It is the ultimate confirmation of non-duality and that the true nature of all things is *Sunyata*. And that everything lacks an inherent, or independent nature (*Swabhava*). Both Nagarjuna and Yogacara's philosophy provided doctrinal foundations, but Zen has in every way developed itself as an independent school with unique characteristics.

Aspects of Zen metaphysics

Zen practitioners look directly into the core teachings of the Buddha but discard all mannerisms of outward presentation by scriptures and scholars [4]. The teachings of Buddha are contained in the doctrines of dependent origination (*Pratitya Samutpada*) and non-substantiality or non-essentiality (*Sunyata*). We know that *Sunyata* is not nothing, but a subtle experiential state of indifference, a state between difference and nondifference. To understand Sunyata is to achieve *Maha Prajna* or supreme wisdom. The knowledge that truth is not in existence or non-existence. But truth is in the consummation of the two extreme positions, the summation of which is the new position of indifference called emptiness. The extreme position is world views, where things are adjudged according to their identification. But it is only a temporary recognition. Understanding Sunyata, one sees the unity in all things.

All unite in nothingness, and it is the only absolute. Mahayanists believe in a transcendental truth (*Paramartha Satya*) that is empty when contrasted with the realness of the phenomenal world [5]. *Paramartha* or absolute truth is mistakenly considered to be *Sunya*. But *Sunya* when taken in its literal sense means a position of void or negative space does not constitute it. *Satya* is *Sunya* because there is no individualization of characters or concepts in it. This is saying that transcendental truth or absolute reality is empty because it is beyond individualization and devoid of innate nature. So, it can neither be *Sunya* nor not *Sunya*, and neither real nor unreal. This is because the above terms are relationships based on similarity and contrast and *Paramartha Satya* is the unifier of all contrasts and concepts. So, any designation of *Sunyata* as either void or empty is misleading. The realness of the phenomenal world should not also be condemned, not that anyone knows that it is conditional, relative, and ultimately unreal. Nagarjuna has cautioned against this oversimplification and abandonment of the sensual world [6]. This would be a rather wrong interpretation of the *Samvritti Satya* or the phenomenal world because doing so could lead to a misunderstanding of the Middle Way.

Although the two levels of truth are not explicitly articulated in Zen, some elements align with Zen's exploration of reality. The emphasis on non-duality and direct experiencing reality as followed in Zen is nothing but the Madhyamika way of understanding beyond conventional truths. Besides, Zen focuses on direct insight through experience that resonates with the spirit of *Paramartha Satya*, which emphasizes that truth cannot be linguistically expressed and conceptually understood. Zen, acknowledges the functioning of a conventional reality, and its validity in everyday life. So much so that, Zen does apply skillful means, language, and scriptural guidance to initiate direct insight.

Emptiness and Suchness

In some sense, there is an individual status assigned to man in Zen, with enough time for man to realize his inner Buddha and extend it to others through compassion. Man is unique such that each individual possesses within him something distinct. While examining the essential nature of all men, one cannot find any inherently existing substance or self-entity. This is Sunyata that challenges the notion of a fixed, or unchanging identity separating sentient beings. In Zen, one way of approaching the state of 'emptiness' is through 'suchness'. In a much deeper understanding, emptiness is often seen as the same as suchness. Suchness or Tathata or Thusness means to see reality as such or just as it is, without superimposing any concepts or percepts whatsoever. Reality is changing, defined momentarily, and constructed relatively. Amidst this ever-changing, impermanent, relative reality, one only tries to fit in. In many ways, emptiness and suchness are complementary aspects of Zen. Emptiness emphasizes the absence of an inherent or independent existence when phenomena are analyzed, and suchness refers to the immediate, unfiltered experience of reality as it is. So, in the Zen way, to see the emptiness in all phenomena is to see the suchness in all.

When the Buddha reached his enlightenment, he set the wheel of *dharma* by acknowledging the 'four noble truths' that envelope human existence from birth to death. The four noble truths correspond to the hard evidence about life and human existence. They are:

- Suffering (*Duhkha*) is there everywhere.
- It is caused by cravings (*Duhkha Samudaya*).
- Suffering can be removed by eliminating causes (*Duhkha Nirodha*).
- The process of elimination of *Duhkha* is the path of *Madhyama Pratipad*.

The first truth speaks of life in every condition characterized by *Duhkha* or suffering, pain, and misery. A man suffers from having no company, being in bad company, and separation from the best company. He inevitably suffers. The second truth gives a justification for *Duhkha*. He suffers because he identifies himself as separate from others (ego gratification). Desires (*Trishna*) and sensations (*Vedana*) are the root cause of all his sufferings because they create an illusion of a separate self that produces activity out of vested interests and demands for more possessions driven by an insatiable thirst for enjoyment. The third truth speaks about emancipation from misery which is possible by destroying all cravings (*Upadanas*). The fourth truth speaks of the eightfold spiritual path (*Ashtanga Marga*) which is the proposed way to Nirvana following which there is a certain end to suffering.

A theory of creation

According to Dr. Radhakrishnan, the creation of life and thus suffering, starting at birth and ending with liberation (*Nirvana*) is the very explanation for *Pratitya Samutpada* [7]. It is the chain of causation as stated by the Buddha himself. It happens on account of ignorance (*Avidya*) that creates impressions (*Samskaras*). From *Samskaras*, consciousness arises, and that results in name (*Nama*) and form (*Rupa*). This gives rise to sensations through the sensual apparatus (five senses and the mind) that gives birth to desires and then to attachments. Attachments result in becoming (*Bhava*) and further result in the birth of life and all suffering along with it. Each factor is dependent on the previous one and this accounts for all interdependent origin. The first cause of this origin theory is *Avidya* (ignorance).

Avidya is both the bearer and breeder of an individual's accumulated karma. The false notion of 'I' or of a separate self is the creation of both *Avidya* and karma. *Avidya* conceals the true nature of life which is sorrow. The more one indulges in this self-pleasing of the needs, the more one accumulates karma. It is the storehouse of all of one's actions along with their motives that leave impressions (*Samskaras*) on the individual consciousness as well as on the collective consciousness [8]. Consciousness is interdependent with name and form. Without a physical body, consciousness cannot proclaim its previous *Samskaras* and without an individual consciousness (subject), there is no world of objects. The doctrine of *Pratitya Samutpada* is the explanation for the origin and working of the whole mass of suffering. Since the doctrine highlights the interdependency and a necessary cause and effect principle, the process can be reversed, and with it suffering ended. When ignorance is destroyed in the complete absence of desires, all *Samskaras* are destroyed and with it, all cessation of suffering is possible.

According to Buddhism, there is no universal substance in anything. So, there is no universal essence of all things which means there is no unifying entity that can explain the creation of all things. All phenomena are related to one another, out of a causal necessity, insofar as they serve a purpose, i.e., the creation of all things.

But their impermanent nature confirms that there is no ultimate source that can be called the first cause of creation. Buddhists reject the notion of an absolute and this forms the core of Buddhist philosophy which is based on the principle of *Anatman* or no self.

The idea of a no-self is a very difficult concept to grasp because of a primary reason called the 'I' consciousness (ego). The ego or the individual self appears to be permanent because of its association with the *Skandhas* that account for all of the individual's memories, emotions ideas, volitions, desires, etc. Buddhists argue that just because there is a conscious identity of the self or the individuality of the ego, does not necessarily mean that there is an *Atman* (soul) as the supreme identity. The primary reason behind this logic is the fact that particular existences are only a result of the various combinations of causes (*Hetu*) and conditions (*Pratyaya*). It exists because they are brought about by the laws of *karma*. *Karma* only serves to sustain the conditions as long as they are conducive. But once the conditions change, because of their very nature, things lose their efficacy, and new things come to replace them. So, there cannot be any irreducible reality of permanent nature, let alone a soul that would defy the notion of impermanence. The Buddhists do not deny the unity of consciousness (*Vijnana*) but only the unifying of the soul (*Atman*). Their denial is the assertion of their belief that there is no unity in absolute and as such it cannot be unconditioned or independent [9].

Primitive Buddhism was convinced of the idea that the Buddha's teachings are contained in the dependent origination theory of causation, four noble truths, and the eight-fold path of virtuous living, *Anatman,* and nirvana. Buddhism is not contained in its doctrinal philosophies.

Although Buddhism has a solid metaphysical foundation, Zen as part of Mahayana Buddhism, believes in understanding the Buddha's message in the living spirit. The mere doctrinal study is the superficial approach that the latter Buddhists opposed after 6th Century CE. Their approach is to understand Buddhism as the Buddha himself did. It means to understand the Buddha's message, one only needs to enrich one's inner consciousness by following the methods of the Buddha. The methods are not a means to an end, neither are they end in themselves. Rather they are tools with rich content that penetrates the barrier of inner consciousness. And when one grasps the full potential of this inner consciousness, one may attain nirvana.

There is no secular metaphysical system proposed in Zen. But in saying so, metaphysics cannot be denied in Zen. At least not in the stage of admission to its practice. Zen Buddhists refer to the occasional reading of the scriptures, primarily among which are the *Lankavatara sutra*, and *Prajnaparamita* texts like *the Vajrachhedika sutra*, *Hridaya sutra*, and *Vimalkirti sutra* of the *Mahayana* tradition. The sutras give information about a very elaborate and logical blueprint of Buddhist metaphysics. Yet the construction and retention of such metaphysical understanding is discouraged in Zen. The idea is to inform the Buddhist mind of the presence of a relative and dualistic reality that the mind falsely perceives as real. Unaware of this truth, the mind dwells in duality mistaking it as reality. Reality on the contrary is the unconditioned stage, where all constructs of the mind are annihilated, so much so that, one remains unaffected by mental worries, conditions, and constructs.

Influence of Taoism and Confucianism

During the initial development of Zen in China

(Chan), reality was depicted as a dynamic and interchanging relational phenomenon. Each phenomenon arises from a preceding one and is followed by another and so on. All things are dependent on each other and this dependence is not as an external condition that binds everything, but an innate nature that interpenetrates through everything making reality a dynamic flow of changes, in a continuous stream of interrelating and interdependent phenomena. This idea has Taoist and Confucian influences too, where the primordial nature of all things is seen as nonstationary, an infinity of relative patterns, and an automatic self-creation. Both believed in the unity of opposites resulting in a fluidity of boundaries between them creating a universal harmony in all things [10]. They also believed in the interconnectedness between shared relationships among individuals, societies, and the natural world, focusing on social harmony among all [11]. Such concepts of interpenetration and relativity resonated well with the Buddhist ideas of interdependence and the impermanent nature of reality and were included in Zen.

What are Koans?

The unique approach to metaphysics in Zen is further amplified through the use of Koans while transmitting Buddha's message. Koans are contradictory statements, enigmatic expressions, or paradoxical questions that are designed to incite contemplation and insight. These are tools used in Zen to transcend conventional thinking and reach a deeper understanding. Koans often lack rational solutions and are skillfully aimed at disrupting the ordinary patterns of the mind. They are also nonsensical statements used to create confusion in the mind by pushing it to think beyond logic. By doing so, one is expected to experience a deeper truth within themselves. It's a deliberate strategy applied to provoke a shift in consciousness and awaken it to enlightenment.

As a result, the self gets affected by spiritual anxiety that creates an overpowering unsettledness within oneself. David R Loy calls it *Ichin* or the doubt sensation [12]. By rigorously engaging with this doubt, without demanding a logical answer or a straightforward resolve to it, one gets to answers by annihilating the very concept of doubt itself. *Ichin* or *Hishiryo* (Japanese) is fundamental to Zen and is a recognized phenomenon important in reaching enlightenment.

What is 'Buddha nature'?

The final goal or enlightenment in Zen is to realize one's true essence which is often referred to as 'Buddha nature' or the 'Original nature'. It awakens the mind to the interconnectedness of all things, resulting in a profound state of clarity about the illusory nature of the self, awareness in each moment, wisdom, compassion, and inner peace [13]. Enlightenment or *Satori* (Japanese), is the pinnacle of spiritual aspiration in Zen, marking the attainment of profound insight and the final liberation from the cycle of suffering.

Satori and stages of progression

In Zen, although not specifically categorized, there are still various accounts of progression to awakening leading up to *Satori*. One of the stages is called *Kensho* or the initial insight. It is often described as a sudden realization or a brief moment of enlightenment offering a glimpse beyond the ordinary perception [14]. It is marked by the awakening to one's true nature. With continuous striving, there comes a stage of further and deeper insight or prolonged awakening. It involves a gradual refinement and integration of the initial experience or *Kensho* into everyday life, resulting in a more balanced and continuous sense of clarity and understanding. A further higher state is that of *Mushin* or no-mind which we have discussed previously in this chapter. It is the transcendental stage of non-discriminatory awareness, where the dichotomy of the subject and object is annihilated leading to no mind [15]. It is the awareness of non-duality, in the absence of all dualistic thinking, where reality is seen as a unified whole. Its realization is paramount in Zen, for realizing the ultimate nature of existence and awakening to enlightenment.

The fundamental belief in Zen is that its way is the transmitted essence of the Buddha's life itself encoded in his teachings. Zen through its integrated metaphysical system, unveils a reality that is beyond words, concepts, ordinary experience, and reason. It's a reality of unbound existence, with each aspect in an interdependent and interconnected relationship with one another. It also refers to the awakening of the individual, by dissolving the barriers of ego and embracing the unity underlying the divisions. The individual comes to a profound realization that he is not different from others, either in identity or in worth emits wisdom, and embodies compassion and a sense of harmony with the universe. The metaphysics in Zen is an invitation to transcend the limitations of the conditioned mind leading to a holistic recognition of one's true self. The metaphysical goals in Zen are achieved in two part process. Firstly, it proposes a shift in consciousness to unearth insights that surpass the limitations of intellect and language. It does so through employment of Koans, and the cultivation of no-mind. Secondly, it challenges us to transcend all dualistic thinking and directly perceive the true essence of reality. One can do so by embracing the interplay between emptiness interconnectedness and interdependency among all phenomena. This is not mere philosophical explanation, but a lived experience, that uncovers the true nature of one's self, and the truth about reality.

3.2 Metaphysics in Advaita Vedanta

Advaita Vedanta marks a great shift from the theism of the Vedas to the intellectual realism of the Upanishads. Vedanta, or the end portion of the *Vedas*, which are the Upanishads, is only the enriched version of the central teachings of the *Vedas*. The Upanishads, represent themselves as the final goal of the *Vedas*, and also are meaningful in essence [16]. Vedanta is often accepted as the perfect system in Hinduism and is followed by more than a billion people around the world. Advaita Vedanta is a significant branch of Vedanta, that was revamped around the 8th century CE.

Every system of Vedanta is derived from three texts (*Prasthana-Traya*). They are: (i) Upanishads, (ii) Bhagavat Gita, and (iii) Vedanta Sutras or the Brahma Sutras. The Upanishads themselves are *Sruti* (revelations) and the Gita and the *Brahma Sutra* are *Smriti* (compositions). The Upanishads are the primary texts for Vedanta and the other two are based on the Upanishads. The system of Vedanta is two-folded, namely, absolutistic and theistic. Absolutistic because it celebrates the eternality of the *Vedas* and accepts that the *Vedas* are *Apurushaya*, i.e., not written by any mortal man. And theistic because Vedanta affirms that the *Vedas* are transcriptions and recordings of divine revelations, revealed to sustain 'reason' and address the needs of humanity. Advaita Vedanta is of the former type, where, a shift was witnessed from the external ritualistic worship of the 'elements' to the internal subjective introspection and subsequent identification with the eternal 'substance'. The system of Vedanta, which was popularized by Sri Adi Shankaracharya is Advaita Vedanta, which is the non-dual or absolutistic school of Indian Philosophy. According to P. Nagaraju Rao, Advaita Vedanta is a way to experience the spirit and explain it through logic. Shankaracharya's Advaita Vedanta employs rigorous logical analysis, drawing from the Upanishads and the Brahma Sutras.

Scriptures are the initial source

Advaita Vedanta credits the scriptures as the original source for its philosophy. The authority of scriptures is not taken for granted. That means anything that can be known through perception or inference does not need scriptural authority. To perceive beyond the senses, one needs a correct interpretation of the original scriptures and selective writings. The two most important concepts addressed while interpreting the scriptures, particularly the Upanishads, are *dharma* and *moksha*, and the correct way to uphold the former and realize the latter. The primary belief in Advaita Vedanta is that senses and reason, are insufficient to have a complete understanding of reality. The initial authority for Advaita Vedanta is *Sruti* (scriptural knowledge), but the final authority is *Anubhuti* (spiritual experience).

Indispensable pointers in Advaita Vedanta

The central tenets in Advaita Vedanta can be stated as '*Brahma Satyam Jagan Mithya Jiva Brahmaiva Naparah* '[17]:

1. Ultimate Reality is the same as Brahman
2. The world (*Jagat*) has an apparent manifestation in it.

3. The soul (*Atman*) is non-different from *Brahman*.

Advaita Vedanta might seem confusing and paradoxical, and understandably so, because, on one hand, it claims that *Brahman*, is beyond the sphere of all predictions, to the extent that it cannot be described in any positive terms. Yet *Brahman* is equated as being the essential substance that shapes reality. Another confusion may arise while trying to describe *Brahman*. As stated earlier, it cannot be described in positive terms like the question 'What is it?' Rather, it can be described as 'What it is not', i.e., in negative terms, to a certain extent. It is the ultimate source for all things living and nonliving, yet it cannot be described empirically. Any attempt to describe *Brahman* will lead to contradiction and *Brahman* only represents unity in the absolute sense. But to say that *Brahman* cannot be described, does not mean that it does not exist. It is not nonexistence. It can only be known indirectly but realized directly through spiritual experience [18].

What is the definition of Brahman?

Shankaracharya provides two types of definitions to describe *Brahman*.

1. *Svarupalakshana*- This is the essential nature of *Brahman*, i.e., Brahman in essence is *Sat* (existence) - *Cit* (knowledge) - *Ananda* (bliss). But this description can only be understood in negative terms.

That means *Brahman* is not unrealityignorance-sorrow. Existence-knowledgebliss are not distinct qualities of *Brahman*, because Brahman is *Nirguna* (attribute less). But one may understand *Brahman* as 'that' which is existence, knowledge, and ultimate bliss.

2. *Tatasthalakshana*- The first type suggests that the

definition of *Brahman* is selfevident. It does not require any validation. Any attempt to describe it directly will lead to contradiction. But Shankara also suggests that there are certain 'pointers', which although not essential characteristics in the course of realization, only serve to discriminate the objects of duality and help in understanding the concept of a unified *Brahman*. These are not 'biased' pointers, because they are not originally related to *Brahman*. One approach is to employ the method of negation or *'Neti Neti'* to describe Brahman. This method involves rejecting any attributes or qualities that are limited and impermanent to identify the true nature of Brahman. For example, the boundaries of space and time are incapable of comprehending Brahman. The objects of the material world exist within the spacetime continuum, and by nature are limited and impermanent. So, by definition, Brahman cannot be described as something that is changing, transient, and finite.

Shankara accepts the authority of *Sruti* (revealed scriptures), and through it, he admits that a logical hypothesis on the doctrine of *Brahman* can be formulated and then defined. The authority of *Sruti* allows one to grasp Brahman's reality through *Jnana* or knowledge and experience rather than using any sensory apparatus. So, Brahman is real because there is knowledge about it revealed from the scriptures which themselves are divine revelations.

The doctrine of Brahman

Unlike his predecessors and all his contemporaries, Shankara's definition of *Brahman* is not based on a creation theory, because *Brahman* does not create the world. Shankara's idea of *Brahman* is also not a transformative theory, because *Brahman* plays no part in the transformed world. Brahman is both *Aparinami* (not resulting) and *Kutastha* (unchanged). Shankara's definition is neither based on *Arambha* nor *Parinama*, but based on *Vivarta*. The causation theory proposed by Adi Shankaracharya is called *Vivartavada*. The theory proposes a one-way causal relationship between the world (*Jagat*) and *Brahman*. *Brahman* is certainly the cause of the world, but the world is certainly not the product of *Brahman*. It is only an appearance. *Brahman* is the foundational reality, from which the world arises. Without *Brahman*, there is no world. Here, only the cause is independent of the effect, but it is not the other way around. The non-existence of the world does not affect the existence of *Brahman*. According to *Vivartavada, Brahman* only appears as the world (*Jagat*), an individual soul (*Jiva*), and *Isvara* (personal God). The effect is an illusionary manifestation of the cause. So, the world of appearances (effect) does not affect *Brahman* (cause).

What is Maya?

Shankara's explanation for the illusory appearances of Brahman is contained in *Maya*. The doctrine of *Maya* holds such prominence in the system of Advaita Vedanta that some critics criticize Shankara's *Advaitavada* as being a hidden dualistic school, the dual realities being *Brahman* and the world created by *Maya*. But the very word Advaita means non-dual. It affirms that there is only one reality, which is the immutable *Brahman*. *Maya* is the potential of *Brahman*, through which '*Brahman*'s manifestation into the world is possible.

Shankara describes *Maya* as veiled ignorance. It is beginningless, but it has a locus and has contents. In *Adhyasa Bhasa*, Sankara suggests that *Maya* is coeval to life [19]. It is life itself. Just as one cannot say with certainty, when one had the first cognition that he is alive, similarly there is no flash point for ignorance. One is never disillusioned consciously, but one can exercise a conscious decision to get out of this illusion. Ignorance is from the perspective of an individual (locus) and it is about something (content). But *Maya* is not eternal, although it is beginningless. The positive aspect of *Maya* is that, from the individual's perspective, it can be removed by attaining *Brahmanvidya*. Shankara considers the locus of *Maya* to be the individual soul (*Jiva*) and its content to be *Brahman* because *Maya* is *Brahman* in appearance. It exists so long as the *Jiva* identifies with *Nama* and *Rupa*. However, it is annihilated in the process of acquiring *Brahman Chetana*.

The function of Maya is twofold.

1. It veils (*Avarana*) the real nature of Brahman.
2. It shows an apparition (*Vikshepa*) in its place

Maya conceals *Brahman*, and in its place shows the world. It cloaks the ultimate reality and projects an apparent reality. But *Maya* also has a positive side to it, which is its projection as reality itself, it is of the nature of *Bhava Rupa* (positive nature) [20].

Three stages of reality

Shankara's *Advaitavada* at its core is realistic in nature. Reality as such is graded in three stages. These stages are realized only in degrees. They are:

1. *Paramarthika* (absolutely real)

2. *Vyavaharika* (relatively real)

3. *Pratibhasika* (unreal)

Only *Brahman* is absolutely real. Dreams and illusions are unreal. The world of objects is neither real nor unreal. It is objectively real. This domain of reality, Shakara calls '*Mithya*' and by which Shankara means that the world is different from the real and unreal. It is different from the real because the world is not perfect and its contents are eternal. Only *Brahman* could be said to be so. The world is also not unreal, because, it is the result of the collective cognition of all sentient beings. The world is cognized. In terms of determination of the reality of the world, Shankara says it is *Anirvacaniya* (undetermined), which means that it is impossible to determine the reality of the world in the empirical sense and call it either 'real' or 'unreal'.

To someone not believing Advaita, the doctrine of *Maya* may seem like an accepted compromise for the inability to give an exact account of the relationship between the *Brahman* and the *Jagat*. But it is not true, because it is impossible to give a firsthand account for the same. There is no intelligible understanding of *Brahman*, only experiential realization of it. According to Bertrand Russell, all human knowledge is uncertain, inexact, and partial [21]. So, with limited knowledge that is also uncertain and incomplete, it is not possible to empirically devise a relation between *Brahman* and the world.

The world according to Shankara, is the world of objects and not the world of subjects. It is objective in nature and is not a subjective fantasy. It is an illusion, but it is not a dream or delusion. It is the workstation for the individual soul (*Jiva*), where the *Jiva* discovers its relationship with the eternal soul (*Atman*), through direct spiritual experience.

According to the words of S. Radhakrishnan, the doctrine of *Maya* serves a definite purpose, which is embedded in the fact that the world does not have a self-explanation for itself. But it does have a phenomenological character to it. And this character is brought about by '*Maya*'. Besides, *Maya* gives a rational explanation for the 'reality in the appearance' aspect of the world. *Maya* is the potential power of *Brahman* such that *Maya* and *Nirguna* (unqualified) *Brahman* actualize to *Saguna* (qualified God) *Ishvara*.

What is Avidya?

The doctrine of *Maya* is incomplete without giving an explanation and justification for *avidya* (ignorance). In the chapter, the dual function of the doctrine of *Maya* has already been discussed. *Avarana* (concealment) results in ignorance because the true nature of the absolute gets hidden. Maya is *Vikshepa* (projection) because it also creates a channel for *Brahman* to manifest in *Ishvara* and *Jagat*. For *Ishvara* to evolve, *Maya* acts as the cosmic connection, to evolve from Brahman yet being unaffected by *avidya*, throughout the process. Only the individual soul (*Jiva*), which evolves out of *Ishvara*, is affected by *Avidya*. This is because, the contents of *Avidya* are *Sattva* (light), *Rajas* (activity), and *Tamas* (inertia), commonly referred to as the *Tri Gunas*. And all Jiva or individual souls are composite of the Tri *Gunas*. But the contents of *Maya* are *Sattva* only, because *Maya* is inherently like *Brahman* which is of pure *Sattva*.

Shankara, in his commentary of *Brahma sutra*, suggests that the dream of life is launched upon, by the force of *Avidya* [22]. We can thus infer that the power behind that force is *Maya*, which itself is the power of *Brahman*. He rejects any difference in the understanding of *Maya* and *Avidya* and declares that *Mulavidya* (*Maya*) and *Tulavidya* (*Avidya*) are the same because there are only two aspects of the cosmic illusion, concealment and projection [23].

The concealment results in *Avidya* affected by the *Jiva* only, but the projection results in *Ishvara*, totally unaffected by *Avidya*.

The third axiom established in Sri Shankaracharya's Advaita Vedanta is regarding the concept of *Atman* and its indispensable relationship with *Brahman*. Through its lens, there seems to be a multiplicity of individual souls (*Jivatma*). Within all *Jiva*, there is implicit, a unifying soul (*Paramatma*). So, what only appears as an outward multiplicity, is inherently one. The Vedantic paraphrase, '*Atma Sarvasya Atma*', which translates to 'the self is the self of all', summarizes the essence of Shankara's philosophy. *Jivatma* is the same as *Paramatma*, thus implying the non-dual nature of reality. All limitations, ignorance, and sorrow are conditions of the Jiva. But *Atman* is divine. It is in essence, *Brahman* itself. The primordial nature of *Atman* is eternal bliss. So, *Jiva* is innately divine. But this divinity is concealed because the *Jiva* falsely identifies itself as the individual soul. This is a unique explanation of the relationship of the *Jivatma* with the *Paramatma*. According to Shankara, the relations between man and God are consubstantial in nature [24], which means, a man and God are made of the same substance and in essence, are the same as one another. Man is potentially divine, for divinity is his birthright. This is the reason, Shankara positions the soul on a much higher level than the world. He does not mean the individual soul (*Jivatma*) as the soul, but the unifying soul (*Paramatma*).

Other theories on the relationship between Atma and Brahman

Three other theories are also proposed regarding the

exact nature of relations between Brahman and the soul. All three theories, namely, *Abhasavada, Pratibimbavada,* and *Avacchedavada* were proposed by three prominent disciples of Sri Shankaracharya, who in themselves were great scholars and stalwarts of Advaita Vedanta.

Pratibimbavada (theory of reflection): This theory was proposed by Padmapada who was a follower of Sri Shankaracharya, and belonged to the *Vivarana* school of Advaita Vedanta. This theory suggests that *Brahman* reflects through *Ishvara* because of *Maya*. And further, it is *Brahman* that reflects through the individual soul *(Jiva),* but on account of *avidya,* this time. This theory is proposed with the only aim of proving the identical nature of the 'reflected' as the 'original'. According to Madhusudana Sarasvati, a reflection of someone's face in the mirror, is due to the superimposition of the person's face in the mirror [25]. Thus, proving that it is the person himself who is imposing his face on the mirror to cast his reflection. Similarly, the individual souls which appear to be so, are reflections *(Bimba)* of *Brahman*. As such, it is only on account of this reflection, that the world of appearances seems to be many *(Jiva).* But underlying, there is absolute unity of the *Jiva* (soul) with the *Brahman*.

Abhasavada (theory of false appearances): This theory was proposed by Suresvara who studied directly under Shankaracharya. According to this theory, *Brahman* manifesting through *Maya,* becomes *Ishvara.* But when *Brahman* is misunderstood because of *avidya*, it appears as the individual soul *(Jiva).* The cosmic universe along with all its phenomenal entities, are mere illusions [26]. This means that to the *Jiva*, which is qualified by *avidya,* the world of appearances seems to be real. But, once the *Jiva* realizes *Brahman*, all appearances projected upon it vanish instantaneously. And all that remains, is pure knowledge or an understanding of absolute reality. *Avidya* is both the energy needed and the force required for the creation of the multiplicity of appearances.

This seemingly recognizable appearance (*Abhasa*) is limited in cognition and conception. This appearance form is not identical to the ultimate reality. It is only an appearance of the ultimate reality. 'It is an apparent and fresh eventuality or externalization lasting up to a true realization [27]. This appearance, which we call reality is not real in itself and its status is only that of an 'illusion'. This illusion is nothing but the phenomenal world. Like every other illusion, which seems true until one has a clear vision, similarly, this illusion called the world remains so until one attains the knowledge of true reality.

Avacchedavada (theory of limitation): The third theory was proposed by Vacaspati Misra. He was the disciple of Mandana Misra but is often linked to Shankaracharya by his contemporaries [28]. He was the founder of the *Bhamati* school of Advaita Vedanta. According to this theory, *Maya*, which is the nature of *Brahman*, remains unaffected by both *Ishvara* and *Jiva*, the former being its content and the latter, its locus. This theory emphasizes the limitation of the Brahman in appearance (*Jiva*) which has been explained in terms of the contents in a closed jar, based on the original analogy of space and jar, proposed by Shankara. The space (air) enclosed within a tight jar, becomes one with the space all around (atmosphere) after the jar is loosened. Similarly, the individual soul (*Jiva*) which is limited by *Avidya*, becomes completely merged with the ultimate self (*Brahman*), once it realizes the true nature of reality. Again, the trapped contents (space) of the closed jar do not affect the atmosphere all around. Similarly, the individual experience of the *Jiva* is isolated and does not affect other *Jiva*, the point being any space (air) limited by the jar, does not affect the space (atmosphere) overall. Similarly, *Paramatma*, limited by *Avidya*, takes the shape of an individual soul (*Jivatma*). But this does not affect the other *Jiva*. *Brahman*, which is otherwise unconditional and limitless, is conditioned and limited by *Maya* born out of its nature.

But for Sankara, all theories relating to the exact relationship between the *Brahman* and the *Jiva* find their essence in the fact that '*Jiva* is the unchanging *Brahman* ignorant of its true nature' [29]. This means that the universal consciousness (*Brahman*) manifests as the individual consciousness (*Jiva*). Yet for all purposes, the know-how (details) of this process remains a mystery. What is known though is that *Brahman* materializes in the world (*Jagat*), by its nature (*Maya*). When the individual soul (*Jiva*) identifies and realizes its true self through *Brahma vidya*, it merges and becomes one with *Brahman*.

What is Karma?

All major schools of Indian philosophy sought liberation as the great ideal of man. Shankaracharya's Advaita Vedanta is no different. His emphasis on acquiring the right knowledge (Brahma Vidya), was not merely to satiate his spiritual inquisitiveness. Rather, he sought after knowledge that would enable him to attain and promote the highest state of spiritual evolution [30]. This state is that of oneness with the absolute, fulfilling one's human obligation. In the quest for ultimate knowledge, man takes up to several births and rebirths which are conditioned by *Avidya*. The individuality of *Jiva* is because of a person's karma. Shankara only assumed the law of karma [31]. But he did not put much stress on it, he only emphasized the relationship of choices and activity and its effect on one's karma. Here, the sum total of one's thoughts, actions, and intentions make up for all of one's choices and activities in life. He pointed out that this present life is an accumulated aggregate of past karma. One does not have any control over what life one is born into. But future life is very much dependent on one's present choices and actions he takes. So, it is more important to make the right choices and perform morally apt actions because it is in the present, to avoid building bad karma.

The process of karma accumulation does not stop until one attains the knowledge of the absolute. To gain access to such knowledge, one needs to get rid of *Avidya*. But so long as any choice is made or action is performed with an ulterior motive, one is bound by the laws of karma. But actions like the ones performed without vested interests and with absolute submission to God, result in the purification of mind and clarity of thought. Once in that state, a man should not stop and keep heading towards God until he attains *Moksha* when all the seeds of karma will be consumed and the *Samsara* exhausted.

The idea of liberation

Avidya is the seed of the *Samsara*. The goal of human life is to get rid of *Avidya* and thus get out of *Samsara*. *Samsara* is the cycle of birth and death of the individual soul (*Jiva*). The *Jiva*, because it attaches itself to the modalities and modifications of *Avidya*, qualified by various titles (*Upadhis*), becomes a *Samsara*. A *Samsari* is one, to whom the world appears as real, although it is an illusion hiding reality. *Samsara* binds the *Jiva*, but the *Jiva* is not bound to the *Samsara*. The highest virtue in man is his potential to reach the highest evolution of becoming one with the creator. Man is responsible for his own choices and actions. Bondage is self-creation, so liberation is also self-made. No God can do for a man, as much as a man can do for himself. Man is not just a product of his impulses. His potential is infinite. But his knowledge is limited, and based on an illusion. The sky only gives the impression that it is blue in color. This impression is false but its contents are true because there are various gases and particles combining in the atmosphere resulting in the visibility of a colour we call sky blue. Unless one realizes that the space is ultimately colorless, one is convinced of its blue color. Similarly, *Samsara* is real, insofar as one thinks that the world is real. This unawareness of the truth is the definition of bondage, and its reason is *Avidya*. There is a way out and it achieving it is the highest goal of human life. It is achieved in *Moksha* which is attained through *Jnana*.

What is Moksha?

Moksha is the state of direct realization of something, that has been there all the time, yet there was no awareness of it. This unawareness is the limitation of man. And when the limitation is expanded through *Jnana*, the soul is liberated (*Moksha*) [32]. *Moksha*, a pursuit of liberation, is also an innate desire of man. The finishing end for such a pursuit might be based on the conception of a physical heaven or a wonderful afterlife of sorts. But true *Moksha* is far from pretext. Heaven is on earth, not a place in some imagined future. It is also not the promise of immortality. It is the true state of identification of the self in the present moment [33]. It is the expansion of the consciousness, till there is no further expansion possible and the full potential of human life is realized like the saying, 'A man is truly spent, so that his real worth is revealed'.

Moksha is native to the soul and not derived [34]. It is not externally attained somewhere but is the spiritual birthright of man. It is the reaffirmation of the fact that man is innately divine. The man can rise to true divinity once he realizes his infinite potential. It is the realization of a man, about his true nature. It is the state of being *Jivanmukti* (the state of liberation while still alive). It is the state when one's perception regarding the plurality of the world is corrected, and he understands that he is one with the whole. 'The whole world will be destroyed with the first man attaining liberation' [35]. When the individual realizes that his true nature is identical to Brahman, the illusion of a world and its separateness vanishes and there is no reality that is separate from the absolute (Brahman).

The physical body is bound to decay, but the spirit lingers on. At the time of the death, it is assumed that something like a seed is left behind that creates a new life form. During the death of a person, his acquired senses get absorbed in the *Manas* that eventually merge with the *Prana* (life energy). The essence of all knowledge gained before death (*Nama*) and all personalities assumed in the process (*Rupa*), will be transferred to the next life. In the scale of *Samsara*, karma affects the journey of the soul. Whether a man ascends to divinity or descends to the bottom of the scale will be determined by that person's karma.

The non-dual school of Advaita Vedanta is distinct in the plethora of Indian philosophy because it provides a logical coherence to scriptural interpretation. It also emphasizes transcending the empirical reality to realize the ultimate reality. But more so than anything, Advaita

Vedanta is a highly intricate system that confirms that there is unity of self and Brahman. The way to realize this unity is through Jnana or perfect wisdom. This Jnana cannot be acquired merely from reading the scriptures nor can it be transmitted through testimony, but solely through intuition. It involves expanding consciousness, through deep contemplation and correct interpretation of scriptures. It also involves the transcendence of *Avidya* and all dualistic thinking with it, and recognition of the non-dual nature of existence.

The resultant is the attainment of a state of supreme happiness or absolute bliss, which is not a fleeting emotion but an experience of spiritual fulfillment.

3.3 Comparative Analysis

The two strong currents of Eastern philosophy originating in India, namely Advaita Vedanta and Buddhism, have explored the concept of nonduality like others. The way one generally understands the world is through distinction and recognition marked by difference. One does so to affirm one position over the other. But there will always be two extreme positions of affirmation and negation, and the confirmation of one position is based on the denial of the other. So, there cannot be any independent position for accepting a permanent reality since the notion of something real is a relative adjustment done until the next favorable position is encountered. And reality would be again sandwiched between what is real and unreal, that is between two extremes, projecting a dualistic viewpoint of reality.

In Buddhism, there is no universal 'self' or an absolute reality. Of course, this is an extension and justification for the ultimate position of no-self (*Anatman*) or that of soulless identity. It is the idea that sentient beings lack innate selfhood as there is no soul in individuals. There are only individual egos. The Buddhists go as far as to believe that the emergence of the individual self (*Atman*), or the belief that there is an individual identity for each one of us is the very reason for man's suffering.

The psychological assertions of 'I' or 'Ego' are mere mental figments with no real worth and are only superimposed on reality. The concept of *Anatman* is one of the foundational truths accepted by all Buddhists. It is a revolt against the selfhood in other philosophical systems of its time. Some pin an individual status on the self as in Western philosophy and some 'label' a permanent status to it as a universal entity like in Advaita. But to the Buddhists, the idea of a self is a 'leveling' process that denounces any permanent essence (*Atman*) in all beings.

The Mahayanists often intertwine the no-self (*Anatman*) doctrine with that of *Sunyata* (no inherent identity) and use it to describe the true nature of reality. *Sunyata* is the only possible justification and eventuality for the *Anatman* doctrine. There is a sense of realism in Buddhism. And that sense is that everything is real only in relation to one another. The world is relative because, its contents lack inherent self-nature (*Svabhava*), and only come about when seen through relationships [36].

No individual status can be given to self, or a thing, or any being. This is because a thing is called a thing only because it is in a relationship with other things. Since the world is dichotomous, it can only be observed in terms of identities and recognition. Life gets meaningful because of death since a thing is designated by what that thing is not. To assign a supreme ideal and to substantiate that ideal as the universal 'essence' in all things is absurd to all Buddhists. But the world is still defined at large. It is still caused and produced. This relationship is validated by a theory based on the interdependence of all *Dharmas* (phenomena) called *Pratiyasamutpada* or the dependent origination theory. It is the causational theory of Buddhism but without a creator at the beginning or an 'essence' in its core. A further expansion of this theory happened in China as part of Mahayana Buddhism which set the background for Zen metaphysics. The Chinese Mahayanists belonging to the Hua Yen school accredited the interpenetration of all things along with the original Buddhist theory of interdependence of all *Dharmas*. It is the idea that all phenomena (*Dharmas*) without exception, are in a state of balance with each other, insofar that they are mutually dependent and harmoniously noncontradictory in their interactions. They at all times interfuse onto one another, because of the constant interaction they face.

The conception of *Sunyata*, as a metaphysical truth in Buddhism, is a declaration to non-Buddhists that the world itself is not false. Only the way in which it is interpreted is false. Against this false interpretation of the world, the Buddhists do not propose a new absolute that would supersede all others. They propose subtle assistance for the awakening of man from the false knowledge of a 'creator source' or an 'evolutionary ideal'. The Buddhists were the sharpest critics of Vedic philosophy, which has a supreme source in Brahman. In Zen metaphysics, the above Buddhist ideas are the first reminiscent of reality which is explained in terms of relativity, dependency, impermanence (*Anitya*), and emptiness *Sunyata*.

The doctrine of *Sunyata* is not about an absolute

reality but only specifies the true state of reality which can be understood through *Sunyata* [37]. But there is another term for reality as proposed by the Mahayanists, and deeply accepted in Zen, called '*Tathata*' or 'thusness'. It is the original Buddha nature, the *Prajna* (supreme knowledge), or the realization of *Sunyata*. It is the *Madhyamarga*. The 'thus' in thusness or the 'such' in suchness, is the indication of that nature of reality which bears no vernacular validation and can only be realized directly 'as-it-is'. It is said so because to understand the ultimate reality is to realize that every phenomenon or event is *Sunyata (Nihsvabhava)*. Since reality lacks an 'essential' nature, it can only be explained the very way it is. That's why it is called *Tathata* or exactly as it is [38]. To think of reality as something beyond *Sunyata* is a metaphysical blunder that contradicts Buddha's message and is rejected by all schools of Buddhism including Zen. Reality 'as-it-is', also means, this very moment right here and right now, approached through *Dhyana* which in Zen means complete self-awareness of the moment [39].

One who masters *Dhyana* becomes a *Tathagata* or a Buddha. The affirmation of such a reality is the very justification of an inherent Buddha essence in the core of our being. Unlike the Buddhist revolt of essentialism, here essence means the primordial nature in all sentient beings, which is to become like Buddha. This is called *Tathagatagarbha*, or the womb or the very essence of Buddhahood which is the Buddha nature itself. It is the ability of man who is a physiological and psychological being, to transcend into seeing the true nature of reality as it is. It represents an inner alertness, hidden deep within man, allowing him to potentially experience Buddha nature that comprises reality in its entirety. Man deluded by ignorance, is still capable of realizing the Budha nature.

Tathagatagarbha also represents both the empty and plenty. It is empty of any inherent existence, but at the same time, it is also the capacity for boundless compassion, wisdom, and skillful means to overcome ignorance. The prospects of metaphysics in Zen are borrowed from all sects of Buddhism and other philosophical traditions like Confucianism and Taoism, only to be ditched and completely abandoned for a 'direct realization' of reality that cannot be facilitated by any scriptural authority and masterful testimony.

In Advaita Vedanta, the nondual reality refers to the very idea that veiled beneath the objective reality that is conditional, dualistic, and unreliable, there is a unified, absolute reality called *Brahman*, the one without any second. It also represents the unification of all existence as such. Brahman reality is the one true reality because it is unchanging, attribute-less, eternal, and infinite. *Brahman* is both the material cause (*Upadana Karana*) and the efficient cause (*Nimitta Karana*) of the world. It is to say that all things are modifications of *Brahman*, yet *Brahman* does not transform into the world.

The world only appears real, and its events appear separate and permanent because *Maya* is working. *Maya* which is essential to understanding the metaphysics of Advaita Vedanta, is the reason why *Brahman* appears as many. It is because of *Maya* that sentient beings fail to recognize *Brahman*. This tendency of *Brahman* and the dependency of the world on it is called the *Vivartvada* or the 'illusionary transformation of *Brahman*'. According to this theory, *Brahman* appears as the world (*Jagat*) and souls (*Jiva*). It is a one-sided causal relationship between *Brahman* and the world where *Brahman* is the absolute constant and is nondependent on the world for its recognition. But the world with all its modifications, as *Jiva* (individual souls), *Jagat* (world), and *Ishvara* (God) is thoroughly dependent on *Brahman* for its creation.

The working of *Maya* is timeless and eternal, but unlike *Brahman*, *Maya* is not real [40]. For *Maya* needs a locus (*Jiva*) to work. Its content is *Brahman* since it is powered by it. So, the working *Maya* presupposes *Jiva*. But *Jiva* is not bound by *Maya*. The existence of *Jiva* is the very proof that there is *Maya*. With *Brahman Jnana* (wisdom), the veil of *Maya* can be completely removed. It is a positive phenomenon that is powered by *Brahman* and enforced on the *Jiva*. Yet, without the *Jiva*, *Maya* cannot function. Its dependency on the *Jiva* gives objective relevance to it and hence is a positive content. And its necessity and working is required for the very existence of *Jiva*. That makes it eternal and timeless.

The objective world (Jagat) is *Mithya* (false) according to Advaita Vedanta. The world is also not real and unreal at the same time. What Shankara means is that the world of objects, which is cognized by the *Jiva* has some reality to it such that the apparent nature of the world does not make it worthless. *Brahman* is considered *Nirguna*. But its position in the world is justified as the mover of all things only when it is associated with its qualities and an action is performed. The *Jiva* has a stake in the *Jagat* and participates in it willingly or unwillingly. Even if the Jiva practices complete inaction, it still is breathing and thinking. So, the Jiva is always doing some action. Therefore, the world cannot be absolutely false. It cannot be absolutely real because only *Brahman* is real. So, the world is somewhere in between. It is *Anirvacaniya* (undermined). It appears to be real until the real appears.

Like the world of appearances, the souls also appear to be many (*Jiva*). However, both the *Jagat* and the *Jiva* are the manifestations of Brahman, yet the *Jiva* somewhat occupies a more prominent position in the hierarchy than the *Jagat*. Jiva or the individual soul is actually the empirical ego that appears as many. It is the proof of individuality in man, at least in the physiological sense. However, there is one universal soul (*Atman*) that essentially connects the *Jiva* with *Brahman*. Individuality is a conditioned state of man that hides its permanent nature. When one acquires *Brahman Jnana* the world ceases. The soul, which is bounded by misery, ignorance, and isolation as the Jiva, frees itself and submerges into *Brahman*. This reveals the true nature of the soul, i.e. its identical relationship with *Brahman*.

Unlike the common misconception, Shankara does attach a theory on personal God (*Ishvara*) to his *Advaitavada*. An *Ishvara* is the creation of *Maya*, built in the image of Brahman (attribute less) [41]. The approach to *the* realization of *Brahman* starts with a personal relationship with a God, done through a strictly administered spiritual practice. Traditionalists believe that a deep connection with a personal God is a necessary predisposition required for realizing *Brahman*. Yet there are others who consider that the invocation of a God with qualities is a compromise for the inability of the lesser minds to comprehend an impersonal absolute. Either way, the worship of God is a necessary justification for the readiness of the *Jiva* to receive higher wisdom. *Ishvara* is different from the *Jiva* and the *Jagat*. The *Jiva* is only capable of creating a subjective world or personal interpretation (individual phenomenon) within *Jagat*, by his own tendency and action. But *Ishvara*, being the near image of *Brahman*, holds the power of *Maya*, and with it can create the objective world or the overall phenomena.

The relativity and objectivity of the world are created by *Ishvara* through the working of *Maya*, all originating from *Brahman*.

Every religious doctrine has contained within it a highest principle that gives substantiality to the religion and a supreme goal that gives meaning to its following and practice. In Advaita Vedanta, the indubitable principle is *Brahman* and the goal is to attain *Moksha* (ultimate liberation). This very conception is the justification for man's suffering and misery. *Avidya* (ignorance) is the starting point of life as we know it. It can only end in *Moksha*, which is the way out of all suffering. It is the final destiny of man, perused life after life and birth after birth until attained. According to Shankara, *Moksha* is the affirmation of the confirmation in the unity of the soul and *Brahman* [42]. The limitations of the individual soul are surpassed by the attainment of *Moksha*. *Moksha* is not seen as an impossible dream or distant reality. It is achievable, because of the innate divinity in man. A part of the realization of Brahman is the truth that man is dearly closer to the creator. The closest one can get to the *Brahman* realization is while living not after death. It is achievable here and now.

The one who achieves *Moksha* is called a *Jivanmukta*. Prof. Nagaraju Rao says that a *Jivanmukta* is a living example of a realized soul in Advaita Vedanta. A *Jivanmukta*, reveals his acquired knowledge to others and not just keeps it to himself. It's what the realized soul does after his enlightenment. He bears the flagship for compassion and love. He does not become immortal but is unaffected by the very notion of mortality. He becomes the living exemplar of the highest possible living of a non-dual reality. Unaffected by the social constraints entitled to him, he becomes a divine incarnate, not to perform miracles but to lead the way for others to believe and follow.

A similar account is available in Zen, with the same spirit. An individual aspires to achieve the awakening and vows to help others attain enlightenment before he reaches his own, out of pure love and compassion. He is called a Bodhisattva. Besides, a Bodhisattva also prioritizes the welfare of all sentient beings expressing his altruistic motives. In Zen, the Bodhisattva ideal is understood as the same thing as realizing the Buddha-nature. The Bodhisattva practices of skillful meditation, mindfulness, and compassionate action resonate well with the Zen practices. The Bodhisattva path in Zen Buddhism is a testimony for the Zen followers to fully engage themselves in the world, remain mindful in each moment, and become compassionate in every action while cultivating insight and striving for enlightenment.

Despite being two different approaches to experiencing the true nature of self and reality, and attaining enlightenment, both Zen Buddhism and Advaita Vedanta converge on the understanding of non-duality. Although different ways, both assign similar boundaries to conceptual understanding and dualistic thinking, with ample room for transcending them, by directly apprehending reality. Beneath the sheath of a conditioned and relative version of reality, which man so dearly clings to, there is the revelation of an indivisible truth. Both traditions are proposed ways to recognize this truth.

References

1. *Zen Buddhism: Selected writings of D.T Suzuki, William Barrett, Page-3*

2. *The Way of Zen, Alan Watts, Page-47*

3. *Buddhism: Its essence and Development, Page162*

4. *The Way of Zen, Alan Watts, Page-77*

5. *Outlines of Mahayana Buddhism, D.T Suzuki, Page-96*

6. *Ibid-Page-97*

7. *Indian Philosophy (Vol-1), S. Radhakrishnan, Page-346*

8. *Outlines of Mahayana Buddhism, D.T Suzuki, Page-35*

9. *Ibid, Page 41*

10. *The Tao of Zen, Ray Grigg, Page 184*

11. *Ibid, Page 185*

12. *Nonduality: In Buddhism and beyond, David R Loy, Page 173*

13. *Zen Buddhism: Selected writings of D.T Suzuki, William Barrett, Page 97*

14. *Ibid Page 121*

15. *Nonduality: In Buddhism and Beyond, David R Loy, Page 21*

16. *Indian Philosophy (Vol-2), S. Radhakrishnan, Page-398*

17. *Critical Survey of Indian Philosophy, Chandradhar Sharma, Page- 273*

18. *Introduction to Vedanta, P Nagaraja Rao, Page-119*

19. *Ibid-Page-132* 20. *Ibid-Page-129*

21. *Ibid-Page-134*

22. *Indian Philosophy (Vol-2), S. Radhakrishnan, Page-536*

23. *Critical Survey of Indian Philosophy, Chandradhar Sharma, Page-274*

24. *Introduction to Vedanta*, P Nagaraja Rao, Page- 138
25. *Bhamati and Vivarana School of Advaita Vedanta*, P.S. Roodurmum, Page-138
26. *Ibid*- Page- 136
27. *Ibid*-Page-137
28. *Ibid*-Page-139
29. *Indian Philosophy (Vol-2)*, S. Radhakrishnan, Page-568
30. *Hinduism*, Troy Wilson Organ, Page-266
31. *Indian Philosophy (Vol-2)*, S. Radhakrishnan, Page-592
32. *Ibid*-Page-593
33. *Ibid*-Page-594
34. *Introduction to Vedanta*, P Nagaraja Rao, Page-144
35. *Indian Philosophy (Vol-2)*, S. Radhakrishnan, Page-594
36. *The Way of Zen*, Allan Watts, Page-63
37. *Madhyamika Sunyata: A Reappraisal*, G.C Nayak, Page-20
38. *Ibid*-Page-33
39. *The Way of Zen*, Alan Watts, Page-55
40. *Introduction to Vedanta*, P Nagaraja Rao, Page-129
41. *Ibid*-Page-139
42. *Ibid*-Page-144

Chapter 4

Epistemology

4.1 Introduction

Epistemology is the philosophical inquiry of knowledge. It explores all questions about knowledge, including what qualifies as knowledge and what are the limits of knowledge, delving deep into its origin, nature, and validation. It could also be seen as a method for understanding the relationship between the knower and the known, or the subject and the object, within whose boundaries our reality exists.

Western epistemology is deeply rooted in ancient Greek philosophy. Epistemic inquiry in the twentieth century was mostly propelled by the scientific revolution, emphasizing empirical observation and experimentation to understand natural phenomena. Contemporary epistemologists focused on pragmatism to justify knowledge based on the practical consequences of human beliefs. Naturally, the inquiry is done through the analysis of language and the application of logic. From the Eastern perspective, however, criticism is directed at Western epistemology, for its tendency to prioritize rationality and empirical justification overlooking other potential ways of knowing like intuition, emotion, and the relational aspect of the unknown, the known, and the knower.

The fundamental aspect of the epistemological study in Eastern philosophical practices is the recognition and acknowledgment of the limitations of the human mind and its understanding through reason. It declares that the true nature of reality is impossible to comprehend because of the limitations of our senses and intellect. It emphasizes the importance of direct experience, intuition, and introspection in the pursuit of knowledge. In traditions like Zen Buddhism and Advaita Vedanta, the notion that our ordinary way of perceiving reality through our senses and intellect is limited is consistently maintained. Our sensory experience and intellectual faculties not only hold us from the truth about reality but also project a constructed version of it, which man falsely believes to be true. Our understanding is further confined by the limitations of language, and dualistic thinking.

In the metaphysics chapter, we have already learned that Zen Buddhism emphasizes transcending all rational thoughts into a direct experience of the truth because vernacular expression is insufficient to fully understand reality. The concept of Maya in Advaita Vedanta suggests that the reality that is perceived is an illusion and the true nature of reality is beyond the grasp of ordinary cognition. The common theme in both traditions is that our senses and intellect are useful insofar that they help us navigate life into a better life, but are insufficient tools to grasp the ultimate truth about existence.

In Buddhist *Pramanavada or* theory of knowledge, there are only two accepted *Pramanas*, namely, *Pratyaksha* and *Anumana*. *Pratyaksha* (perception) is a way to experience direct knowledge about the world. This condition in Buddhism is known as '*Pratyaksha prastha bhava*' [1]. This statement refers to the state, in which the knowledge gained through direct perception, is the foundational source of knowledge. But, *Anumana* (Inference) is used to conclude the knowledge already obtained about the world. However, such knowledge is limited owing to the changing nature of reality in Buddhism. So, in a much broader pool of methods of understanding reality, both Pratyaksha and Anumana come with their limitations and relevance. The knowledge that is sought in Buddhism, comes through a personal insight that is rooted in direct experience and intuitive understanding. Zen Buddhism's approach to epistemology is based on methods of insight, intuition, and certain *Upaya* that result in having such an experience.

Advaita epistemology or Advaita-Vidya is the process of understanding Brahman by transcending all ordinary ways of thinking. This is because Brahman cannot be grasped through intellectual understanding alone, and requires realization through a direct experience of it. In this journey, a seeker will be continuously challenged and opposed by his reason to reject the notion of one all-pervading entity called Brahman. This realization is a two-part process in Advaita Vedanta. First, it stresses the need to understand the external world, its relationship with the Jiva, and its ultimate status. For this Advaita Vedanta accepts six sources of knowledge, namely *Pratyaksha, Anumana, Upamana, Shabda, Arthapatti,* and *Anupalabdhi*. The second part of realization involves the abandonment of all knowledge acquired through reason, for a higher understanding through intuition. Advaita Vedanta aims to use the above avenues to reach a deeper comprehension of the non-dualistic reality (Advaita) in Brahman.

4.2 Epistemology in Zen Buddhism

In the introduction part, we have already highlighted that Zen Buddhism does not explicitly prescribe to the traditional Buddhist epistemic components. Rather it emphasizes an intuitive understanding of the self, through an intense inward journey. Traditional Buddhism however, recognizes two types of *Pramana* or the means of valid cognition (*Pratyaksha* and *Anumana*) with an emphasis on understanding the three facets of existence- namely, non-self (*Anatman*), impermanence (*Anitya*) and Suffering

(*Duhkha*). All epistemological investigations are directed mostly at understanding these facets directly, for which it applies various *Upaya* or skills like meditation, logical reasoning, and scriptural studies. Before understanding the epistemology that Zen subscribes to, it would be helpful to get a familiarity with traditional Buddhist epistemology, so that it would give a simple picture of what is abandoned in Zen and what is accepted by it in its quest for the truth.

4.2.1 Pratyaksha

In traditional Buddhist epistemology, knowledge can be either perceptual or inferential and hence there can be only two valid sources of knowledge or types of *Pramana* called *Pratyaksha* and *Anumana*. This forms the foundation for the twofold theory of knowledge in Buddhist epistemology. In the Buddhist tradition, the word '*Pramana*' means both the process by which knowledge can be acquired and the knowledge gained in that process. The Buddhists do not distinguish between *Pramana* as a process of knowledge and *Prama* as a result of that process. For Buddhists, the act of cognizing is the same as the cognition of an object. *Pramana* to the Buddhists means, that by which an object is known, *Pramiyate artha aneneti*.

According to the Buddhists, there can only be two kinds of objects of knowledge (*Prameya*), namely, *Svalakshna*, or the unique particular characteristics, and *Samanyalakshna*, or the generalized mental image or construct of the mind. The first kind is the ever-passing 'moment' which is unique and is in a continuous loop of preceding and subsequent moments. In that sense, each moment is incomparable with another and is distinctly real from other moments. Such a reality is momentary and yet dynamic. This is a reality in itself and cannot be named. To name it is to call it real and hold it for more than a moment. And reality as such is momentary.

The constructs of the mind, however, project a more generalized version of reality called *Samanyalakshna,* or the shared version of reality that is shaped by our thoughts in the mind. This common version is formally imposed by the mind. Since there are only two kinds of objects of knowledge, namely, the *Svalakshna* and the *Samanyalaksana,* there can be only two kinds of knowledge gained, one corresponding to each. *Svalakshna* corresponds to perceptual knowledge or *Pratyaksha* and generalized mental constructs or *Samanyalaksana* corresponds to inferential knowledge or *Anumana.*

Pratyaksha or perception is pure sensation or the direct contact of senses with a unique particular. *Anumana* or inference is a mental construct in the form of a mental image. By this implication, objects that can be perceptually understood can never be comprehended by inference and vice versa. Such positioning of mutually exclusive modes of knowing is called *Pramanavyavastha*. *Pratyaksha* is considered a foundational *Pramana* and inference depends on it.

Based on available information, Vasubandhu of the fourth century CE can be considered the first Buddhist epistemologist. In his famous book *VadaVidhi,* he defines *Pratyaksha* as *'Tatorthad Vijnanam Pratyaksham',* which translates to 'Perception as that cognition produced by that particular object'. While defining perception, Vasubandhu gives more importance to the role of the object (*Alambanapratyaya*) over the role of cognitive senses (*Adhipatipratyaya*) or the cognizing consciousness (*Samanantarapratyaya*). For Vasubandhu, the bare experience of an object without any conceptual elements is perceptual cognition [2] For example, if the object is fire, then it can be known through perceptual cognition because the object is real. But to have an idea of fire, we have to associate it with some mental construct based on memory or judgment. For example, a 'hill on fire', or a 'smoky mountain' are inferential cognitions.

Unlike Vasubandhu who defined *Pratyaksha* in positive phraseology, the other two primary Buddhist epistemologists Dignaga and Dharmakirti used negative phraseology [3]. But they both differ in their full rendering of negative phrases they used in the definitions. Dignaga, the fourth-century CE philosopher, gives a specific method of defining *Pratyaksha* using double negation called *Atadvyavrtti*. For him, a definition is only a negative characterization (*Vyavrtti*), i.e., 'what it is not'. He defines *Pratyaksha* as that which is not a *Kalpana* (conception). *Kalpana* stands for both thought and speech. So, *Pratyaksha* is *Kalpanapodham* [4], which is another way of saying that *Pratyaksha* is nonconceptual and non-verbal. According to him, sense perception is the first moment of every cognition. The basic feature of cognition is that it is always new because every instance is momentary. So, all things perceived are unique and immediately given to us in experience.

Dharmakirti, the sixth-century CE Buddhist thinker, continues from Dignaga's definition and defines *Pratyaksha* as '*Kalpanapodham Abhrantam*', i.e., the cognition that is non-conceptual and necessarily non-erroneous [5]. In other words, *Pratyaksha* is pure sensation and is only to be experienced and not designated. While explaining the term '*Abhrantam*', Dharmakirti gives examples of different instances of errors that can be caused by color blindness, rapid motion, traveling in a boat, mental sickness, and so on. These causes, whether located in the sense organ or the object, whether external or internal, affect the cognitive sense and the process of *Pratyaksha*. So, perception is sense cognition that is free and distinct from all forms of illusory sensations.

The Buddhist thinkers of the *Vijnanavada* tradition, unanimously insist that *Pratyaksha* is *Nirvikalpa* because it is pure sensation and cannot be determined by mental constructs. So, *Nirvikalpa* is the basic nature of *Pratyaksha*. But in his book *Pramana Samucchaya*, Dignaga classifies four types of *Pratyaksha* which Dharmakirti later elaborates more precisely in his books *Nyaya Bindu* and *Pramana Vartika* [6]. They are:

1. *Indriya Pratyaksha* is the sensation caused by external objects. There are five *Indriya Pratyaksha*, each for one cognitive sense.

2. *Manasa Pratyaksha* is cognition caused by the mind, i.e., the awareness of the cognitive senses.

3. *Svasamvedana Pratyaksha* is the immediate experience of both *Indriya* and *Manasa Pratyaksha*.

4. *Yogi Pratyaksha* is the intuition apprehended by a practicing *yogi*.

4.2.2 Anumana

The Buddhist theory of *Anumana* is developed as the other half of the two-fold understanding of reality. Each *Pramana* corresponds to a particular object of knowledge, namely, the perceptual knowledge through *Pratyaksha* is immediate in experience, and the inferential knowledge through *Anumana* is of the mediating type. When thoughts get associated with the object, and categories are formed, mental concepts are produced, and then reality is shaped. *Anumana* is a *Kalpana* (supposition) which is based on another *Kalpana*. It is used to form a new hypothesis based on existing and recurring facts, analysis of patterns, and formation of judgments based on discrimination. Any knowledge gained through *Anumana* is necessarily judgmental. This is because *Anumana* means mental process based on the knowledge that follows (*Anu +Mati*). A judgment is made on facts that are based on previously known facts. That means *Pratyaksha Jnanam* or perceptual knowledge precedes *Anumati Jnanam* or inferential knowledge.

The Buddhist epistemology is intricately intertwined with the Buddhist system of logic which has the same constituents as the other Indian logical systems, namely, *Paksha* (Subject), *Hetu* (Reason) or *Linga* (Mark), and *Sadhya* (Predicate). *Linga* and *Hetu* is the bridge that connects the *Paksha* with the *Sadhya*.

- *Paksha*: It is the subject that is to be inferred. By definition, *Paksha* is the underlying substratum (*Dharmin*), which has a *Sadhya* and a *Hetu*. Both *Sadhya* and *Hetu* are called *Dharmas*. This means, any subject, while being inferred, will necessarily have a logical relation with certain facts. Therefore, according to Dharmakirti, *Paksha* is defined as '*Jijnasita Visheso Dharma*' [7].

- *Hetu* or *Linga*: It is the reason through which a desired and new conclusion is reached. Similarly, *Linga* is the means that leads to the result, previously unknown. It is also called *Sadhana* because it leads to the *Sadhya*.

According to Dignaga, *Hetu* is a property of *Paksha* that is pervaded by the *Sadhya* [8]. This means *Hetu* is that property of *Paksha* that is present in the predicate, connecting the two.

Buddhist logicians categorize three types of *Hetu*. They are:

- *Svabhava* (Identity) *Hetu*: It is a type of *Hetu* whose mere existence confirms the *Sadhya*. For example, 'This is a cow. Therefore, it is an animal'. The genus cow is sufficient to infer that it belongs to the animal species.

- *Karya* (Effect) *Hetu:* It is the *Hetu* that shares a causal relationship with the *Sadhya*. This relationship describes the effect only, hence the name. This means, if there is an effect, then there must be a cause. While the contrary may not be true always. For example, the sight of smoke means there is fire.

- *Anupalabdhi* (Non-cognition) *Hetu:* It is the *Hetu* that explains the non-existent nature of something. For example, a jar not found in a 'particular place', when looked for it. A jar can be visibly cognized to be at any place and anywhere. But when 'not present' in a particular place, it is non-cognizable in that particular place. This is the nonexistent nature of the jar, which is inferred through *Anupalabdhi Hetu*.

The third element of the inferential process after the *Paksha* and *Hetu* is called *Sadhya*.

- *Sadhya* or *Linga*: It is the property that is to be inferred in the *Paksha*. It is the preestablished condition of the *Paksha* that is to be found out through *Hetu* or *Linga*.

According to Dharmakirti, there are two secondary constituents in the inferential process, namely, *Sapaksha* and *Vipaksha)* [9].

- *Sapaksha*: It is a condition similar to the *Paksha* because both share a common *Sadhya*. For example, 'A hill is on fire because smoke is rising from it. In this statement, smoke is the *Hetu*, fire is the *Sadhya* and hill is the *Paksha*. Therefore, any other place whose property is fire can be called a *Sapaksha*. For example, Volcano.

- *Vipaksha*: It is a condition dissimilar to both *Sapaksha* and *Paksha*.

According to Dignaga, any inferential judgment is based on two primary grounds, namely, *Paksadharmata* and *Avinabhava* [10].

- *Paksadharmata*: It is the relationship between *Paksha* and *Hetu*.

- *Avinabhava*: It is the relation of necessary concomitance between two subsequent facts, where one fact necessarily leads to the other. It is the relationship between the *Linga* and the *Lingin* or between *Sadhana* and *Sadhya*. The *Lingin* is necessarily dependent on the *Linga*. This phenomenon is called *Abhinabhava Niyama*.

For the Buddhists, *Anumana* is a complex cognition, unlike *Pratyaksha* which is cognition as it is. The outcome through *Anumana* is a thought process, divided into constituent parts called *Avayavas*. The entire inferential process when expressed in language, i.e., thoughts converted to words, is called a *Vakya*. In Buddhist epistemology, *Anumana* is the process of concluding a previously unknown phenomenon, based on certain other phenomena, which are used as evidence. It is the logical process of reasoning, wherein, new knowledge is accessed from known premises. The theory of inference is an assurance and then reassurance that, knowledge based on reliable reasoning and concrete evidence is valid and justified. It is a method the Buddhists apply to make sense of the world and understand that aspect of reality, which is otherwise discrete and ever-changing.

The two-fold theory of Buddhist epistemology is an overall presentation of how knowledge is acquired and validated within the Buddhist frame of mind. This theory provides a comprehensive model for understanding reality through the Buddhist mind, encapsulating the nature of cognition, i.e. through sensory perception (*Pratyaksha*) and inferential judgment (*Anumana*). But Zen takes a distinctive departure from the structural and analytical approach of traditional Buddhism. In Zen, the paradigm changes where the emphasis is drastically shifted towards direct and experiential understanding transcending all limitations of linguistic and logical frameworks. Zen advocates for a non-conceptual understanding and realization of non-dual reality, thus transcending any reliance on the dualistic nature of perception and inference, for an awakening experience called Satori.

What is direct experience?

It is the emphasis on the direct apprehension of reality without the filter of preconceived ideas and concepts. It is facilitated through meditation, which is a very fundamental thing to do in Zen. To meditate in Zen is to allow oneself to observe one's thoughts and perceptions but without any sort of attachment or clinging. The importance of meditation (Zazen) cannot be emphasized more, particularly as the most preferred way to cultivate the mind and facilitate direct insight or experience. It is an act of self-induced discipline to clear all mental clatters and habitual thinking, to allow for a direct perception or bare contact with reality.

What are Koans and Paradoxes and why are they important in Zen Epistemology?

To be able to break the habit of conventional thinking, one needs perfect practice and skillful means. One unique approach in Zen is the use of Koans which are enigmatic and paradoxical statements or questions used to disrupt habitual thinking patterns. Its consistent use in Zen also means it is aimed at achieving a breakthrough in understanding. The primary use of Koans is to push one beyond all conceptual thoughts and into a direct realization. There are often no conventional answers or explanations for koans. Koans are not meant to be solved through conventional reasoning. For Zen recognizes that truth cannot be expressed in words. The ineffable nature of reality is thus to be intuitively understood, for which Koans and other paradoxical questioning serve as efficient pointers.

Another unique way employed in Zen is the use of non-verbal means such as unique actions, gestures, or even silence to transmit a direct understanding from the master to the student. The primary idea that Zen transmits is that in the quest for truth, one proceeds not with definitive answers but with a paradoxical realization that knowing truly emerges from a state of unknowing. Truth lies not in grasping answers which themselves are somewhat flawed because they are constructed in the sphere of dualism. Rather, truth is revealed to the one, who surrenders to the profound mystery of existence itself. When done efficiently, one effectively realizes the truth in Sunyata, which is the fundamental nature of all things.

4.3 Epistemology in Advaita Vedanta

Unlike Buddhism, in Advaita Vedanta ultimate reality has a name, and it is Brahman. At its core, Advaita Vedanta claims to be the process of knowing this ultimate reality and exploring the relationship between the knower, the known, and the process of knowing reality. Brahman is the supreme intelligence which is self-sufficient and self-valid. Through a system of epistemology, Advaita Vedanta intends to show that the reality that is manifested from Brahman is also a superimposition of its true nature. Therefore, the world of manifolds is a false one, and the truth about it remains hidden because of avidya or ignorance. To get rid of this ignorance is to transcend the world and know Brahman directly in experience, through intuition.

It cannot be known through any other way but for self-experience. To translate this very experience into a conceptual and philosophical framework, Advaita Vedanta recognizes six sources of knowledge or *Pramana*. The six *Pramana* namely, *Pratyaksha, Anumana, Upamana, Shabda, Arthapatti,* and *Anupalabdhi*, all of which play a crucial role in understanding the nature of reality and the self. They are complete tools employed by Advaita to filter the truth from the illusion, and further advance the cause of spiritual realization.

Pratyaksha is the process of getting a direct experience through the senses. Beyond immediate or direct experience, *Anumana* and *Shabda* account for the mediating knowledge which in the case of the former is based on drawing conclusions based on logical reasoning and in the case of the latter is based on trustworthy words of a master or reliable sources such as scriptures. To understand abstract concepts that do not offer direct definitions, Advaita uses *Upamana* or comparison. The knowledge about something unknown which otherwise cannot be explained directly, is gained about an already established fact by comparing both to one another. *Arthapatti* or postulation is primarily used to reconcile contradictions when they arise in already established facts. It is resolved by assuming or postulating another condition that helps connect the contradicting facts. Finally, noncontradiction or *Anupalabdhi* offers knowledge about the absence of certain entities, that cannot be directly perceivable or inferable through other sources. It highlights the importance of understanding absence as a valid way to comprehend reality. Let's analyze all six *Pramana* in more detail.

4.3.1 Pratyaksha

Pratyaksha or perception according to *Advaita Vedanta* is both a means of right knowledge (*Pramana*) and a type of right knowledge (*Prama*). As a *Pramana*, *Pratyaksha* is the first in the order of independent sources of knowledge verification, because the knowledge produced by perception, gives a direct presentation of the object to the senses. While the object is being perceived by the senses, the knowledge obtained from such a presentation or arrangement can be valid or invalid. Valid knowledge or *Prama* is defined as the knowledge that is new about the object is free from error in judgment and does not involve recollection of memory. This is because an error ultimately makes the knowledge invalid and a recollection gives nothing new about the object perceived. Thus, valid knowledge in Advaita Vedanta is called '*Anadhigata-badhita-rtha-vishayaka-jnaanam*' [11]. It means that any knowledge can be deemed as valid, only if there is no contradiction to it and it has not been previously known by any other source of knowledge.

However, in the customary sense, perception is defined in terms of sense-functioning and interpreted as stimulation of the senses. The Advaita followers reject this common usage in their definition of perception. According to them, perception as a source of knowledge is the instrumental cause of valid cognition, and this is nothing but pure consciousness and the knowledge of *Brahman* [12]. The world and the body are superimposed on the *Brahman* which is immutable and eternal. On its own, it cannot change the world. It is *Maya* or illusion, through which *Brahman* becomes the cause of the world. All objects are veiled under ignorance (*Adhyasa*). Only with the knowledge of *Brahman*, this ignorance can be removed. Without the intervention of consciousness, neither the subject can perceive anything nor can any object be perceived. *So, Pratyaksha* for Advaita followers in its most pristine sense is immediate consciousness and the knowledge of *Brahman*.

Perceptual knowledge or *Pratyaksha Jnana* is accessed when the object interacts with the subject through interactive tools or mental modes. In the first phase, the mind being the instrument of cognition, creates a mental image of the object which is to say, that the mind takes the shape of the object. In the second phase, the consciousness underlying the object is unraveled and this illuminates the object through the mental modes or *Vritti*. In the final phase, the object consciousness gets associated with the subject consciousness, and thus the object gets perceived. In this entire process, it becomes obvious that the mind plays a very important role besides the senses. The senses on their own don't contribute much to perceiving without the association of the mind. The mind here is broadly divided into three parts. They are:

1. *Pramaata-Chaitanya*, the part within the body of the perceiver
2. *Pramana-Chaitanya*, the part extended to the perceived object, i.e., the means of knowledge
3. *Pramiti-Chaitanya*, the part that coincides with the object, i.e., the perceived object

The Advaita followers maintain that the object perceived is nothing but the underlying consciousness that gets manifested or appears to be so. As such the object has no separate existence of its own apart from the all-pervading consciousness or *Brahman-Chaitanya*. So, in the process of perception, knowledge limited by mental modification in the form of a particular object is not so different from the consciousness limited by objects that can be perceived by particular senses. That is to say that the perception of an object, which on principle is only a superimposition on top of the consciousness limited by the object, is not different from pure consciousness. Therefore, the criterion for the perception according to the Advaita followers is not so much the usability of the sense organs. Rather it is the criterion that consciousness associated with the means of knowledge (*Pramana-Chaitanya*) is not different from the consciousness associated with the object (*Prameya-Chaitanya*).

The scope of *Pratyaksha* in Advaita Vedanta is limited to the presentation of the object towards which the mind is directed, such that the object must be appropriate for perception. This property of *Pratyaksha* is called *Yogyata* or fitness. This particular condition rules out ideas like dharma, right conduct, natural laws, and other features of reality that do not present directly to the mind as objects of perception. So, the scope of perception is not that wide according to Advaita Vedanta since *Pratyaksha* is only a method of common sense that makes the object of search directly presentable, and gives the immediate apprehension of the object. Therefore, any given object's direct presentation is the veridical content in the process of *Pratyaksha* in Advaita Vedanta. *Pratyaksha* as a *Pramana* involves the activity of the sense organs and the contact of the senses with the object. But these are not the chief characteristics of *Pratyaksha*. Rather it is the directness of the knowledge acquired about an object in the perceptual process due to the underlying unified consciousness between both the subject and the object.

4.3.2 Anumana

Perhaps, no other *Pramana Vyavastha* in Indian philosophy has been more discussed than *Anumana* or inferential knowledge. The Nyaya philosophers have put extensive work on *Anumana*. Their treatises on many occasions are accepted by other schools of Indian philosophy. Apart from the followers of *Charvaka*, all other schools of Indian philosophy, both orthodox and heterodox, have accepted inferential knowledge as an independent *Pramana*. The account for inference is vividly described in *Vedanta Paribhasa*, the exhaustive book on Advaita epistemology written by Sri Dharmarajha Dhvarindra. There is a consensus amongst the philosophers that inference or the knowledge of *Anumana* is a cognition that follows or presupposes another cognition [13]. It is the knowledge (*Mana*) that follows another (*Anu*) knowledge. This presupposed knowledge is the knowledge of invariable concomitance or *Vyapti* and it is agreed upon unanimously among all philosophers that without *Vyapti* there would be no case of *Anumana*.

What is *Vyapti*?

The epistemological meaning of *Vyapti* is pervasion [14]. *Vyapti* is defined as the case scenario of the coexistence of the *Sadhya* along with the *Hetu*, and thus, the formation of a universalized principle based on it. For example, in the statement 'Smoke is rising from a mountain because it is on fire', the fiery mountain is the subject, the *Sadhya* which is to be inferred. This inference is derived from the reason (*Hetu*). From experience, one can gather that whenever there is smoke, there is fire. This observation is backed up by previous experience of the above situation on many occasions. Therefore, it can be said that smoke and fire are always seen together. A generalized or a more universal relation can be drawn from this, that whenever there is smoke there is fire. This is the *Vyapti* or the invariable concomitance. However, according to Vedanta Shikshamani, which is a commentary on *Vedanta Paribhasa* by Sri Ramakrishna (son of Dharmarajha Adhvarindra), the relation of *Vyapti* cannot be necessarily said to be the relation between cause and effect [15]. For *Vyapti* to occur, the coexistence of *Sadhya* and *Hetu* is a necessary condition. Otherwise, any principle could be universalized. For example, 'Wherever there is an earth, people are living on it'.

One may ask the question how many observations are required to draw a universal concomitance? The Advaita followers hold the view that the question is unessential. A universal concomitance can be ascertained with only a single observation. But it also has to be proved that there are no exceptions to that observation [16]. This means that under favorable conditions, a single observation is sufficient to find a universalized connection between two universals, for example, between 'fire and smoke'. With the knowledge of *Vyapti, which is* based on previously acquired impressions, new knowledge is gained. As such, the function of the knowledge of *Vyapti* is only to revive those previous impressions. This entire process of first locating the *Vyapti*, then reviving past impressions and finally gaining new knowledge is called inference. From the above, one may then deduce that the entire process of *Vyapti* is only a case of memory or recollection of impressions.

Does the process of inference yield any new knowledge? The Advaita followers hold their ground by saying that it does. According to *Vedanta Paribhasa*, memory is defined as the recollection of past impressions or *Samskara*. The object of *Samskara* can be called the major term *Sadhya*, but an inference is not just a recollection. For inference to take place, the relationship between the middle term *Linga* and the minor term *Paksha* also needs to be defined and this must at all times cooperate with past impressions or *Samskara* [17]. The conclusion or knowledge gained through the process of inference is new knowledge and thus the method of acquiring such knowledge is valid and justified.

4.3.3 Upamana

Upamana or the perception of similarity is an independent *Pramana* different from *Pratyaksha* and *Anumana*. The word *Upamana* is derived from the Sanskrit verb *'Ma'* meaning to measure or to know something and the prefix *'Upa'* means near, towards, or resemblance. According to Monnier Williams dictionary, *Upamana* means resemblance, comparison, analogy, simile, or any object for that matter with which anything can be compared. According to the Apte Sanskrit Dictionary, *Upamana* means resemblance or comparison.

Advaita advocates that there are certain situations where knowledge about the object is gained either through pointing out the similarity, dissimilarity, or uniqueness found in the predicate of that particular phenomenon in comparison with the subject given. This is the process of *Upamana* that is different from direct sensation or *Pratyaksha* or *Anumana*. *Upamana* is a method of obtaining knowledge about an object by comparing it with a fact. This definition by extension caters to all those unexplainable phenomena that are difficult to comprehend and express.

There is a famous example of a cow and a *Gavaya* (wild cow) that explains the concept of Upamana. A man goes to the forest and when he comes across a *Gavaya* there, he compares its similar features with the cow which he has seen back in his village. After identifying similar features, he concludes that a cow is similar to a *Gavaya*. There is a sharp objection from some thinkers who, unlike the Advaita followers, view *Upamana* to be merely a case of *Anumana*. These thinkers propose that the similarity of one object with another can be inferred.

Then there are the Buddhists and the followers of Samkhya, who see *Upamana* as the case of perception or *Pratyaksha*. The original perception that a *Gavaya* is like a cow is sufficient to conclude that it must also be the other way around. However, the Vedanta followers argue that such a conclusion can be drawn only after establishing the similarity between the two objects. They say that perception is only one way of finding the similarity between any two objects. In the case of the cow and the *Gavaya*, it can be concluded that a *Gavaya* is perceived like a cow. But it cannot be the other way around also, because it's not perceived that way. To establish the conclusion that a cow must also look like a *Gavaya*, one has to use *Upamana* as an independent verification source. Hence, it is only fair to say that similarity, in this case, is not known through *Pratyaksha* but rather through *Upamana*.

According to contemporary Advaita philosopher Ananta Krishna Shastri, the reason behind the earlier stand on *Upamana* as an independent *Pramana* is to justify the position of the phenomenal nature of the world (*Jagat*) as completely dissimilar to that of absolute reality (*Nirguna Brahman*) [18]. This position of Sri Shastri is challenged because the world is only a perceived object.

4.3.4 Shabda

'*Shabda*', a Sanskrit term, can be translated in English as a 'sound'. In the world of language, a sound, uttered in a particular and peculiar manner is a coded symbol expressing a 'meaning' assigned to it. This unique sound, whether communicated verbally or non-verbally, is called a 'word'. In the present context, a word or a collective and systematic rendering of words as a valid source of knowledge is known as *Shabda Pramana* or testimony. *Shabda* is the fourth in the list of valid sources of knowledge, accepted in Indian philosophy, except for the *Charvaka*, Buddhist, and *Vaisesika* schools. As far as Advaita is concerned, it is often assumed that its advocacy of *Shabda* as an independent and authentic *Pramana*, is in fact to establish the authority of the Vedas [19]. The Vedas, considered '*Apuruseya*', are not believed to have been written by any mortal. Rather the Vedas are a gift to mankind, through divine intervention. And hence, its authority is justified.

A *Shabda* on its own is a definitive word with assigned meaning, but when spoken or used by a trustworthy person, it is called a testimony. A major portion of someone's overall pile of knowledge about the world is based on testimony, either written or spoken by another person. The intended purpose of a testimony is to convey certain facts to certain people. The intention is to always either 'pass down' or 'spread around' information. And it is often seen that a person believes what he hears. Most of this belief is built around 'trust' [20]. Hence a testimony is the words of a trustworthy person. Since knowledge gained by this process is based on trust, it is very much possible that someone may lie about certain facts. This raises the most important question against the validity of *Shabda*, how authority or testimony can be a genuine source of knowledge because the possibility that someone may be lying or deceiving can never be ruled out.

Most schools deny testimony as a valid source of knowledge because of primarily the following two reasons:

- Testimony, no matter who is giving, is not the same thing as the truth.
- Testimony is not an independent verifying source, because it is either based on *Pratyaksha* or *Anumana*.

The first case scenario is a hustle between an authority claiming to be true and any other verifying source like perception or inference. It has already been proved that not all things perceived or inferred are true. So, by the same logic, if the validity of testimony is discarded, then validity by perception and inference should also be questioned.

There will be some cases of perception and inference that will be false and some true. So, there should not be any problem with accepting the validity of some authority to be true. The validation of authentic sources can be found by the same methods as would any other source of knowledge. One can find the truth by testing it either with correspondence, coherence, practicability, and non-contradiction. Thus, there should not be any problem in accepting authority as a valid source of knowledge, just like perception and inference, because the validity of knowledge, in any case, depends upon other conditions [21]. This answers the second case scenario. If testimony yields new information that has not been otherwise derived from any other source, then it is sufficient reason to label *Shabda* as an independent source of knowledge and not reduce it to any other [22].

One of the most striking features of Indian philosophy is that almost all the schools, in addition to other commonly accepted *Pramana* like *Pratyaksha* and *Anumana*, believe in the authority of verbal or written testimony (*Shabda*) when justifying their respective standpoints. But to rely upon authority does not mean belief in unverified and unreliable sources. According to Advaita, it is maintained that the authority of the Vedas is absolute. They arrive at this conclusion by following the historical peculiarity of the scriptures. The early thinkers who were the first interpreters of the scriptures, must have studied extensively and analyzed them critically. After that, they would have authored various texts and commentaries or spoken orally depending upon the time and audience. And then their works have been passed down from generation to generation through tradition. It's a big 'task and ask' for which the early thinkers and subsequent scholars would have assimilated, discriminated, analyzed, and synthesized this vast knowledge and formed an authoritative quorum.

In philosophy, it is believed that any testimony is tested and verified exactly like any road sign [23]. As long as any testimony yields sufficient information for the hearer which is new, it is an independent source of knowledge. Advaita illustrates a beautiful example to explain the authority of a testimony. Ten people were crossing a river. After crossing it, they start to count the number of persons who have successfully made it to the other shore. Every time a counter makes a count, he misses himself and counts to a total of nine, so that one person remains missing all the time. This problem is solved when another passerby counts them correctly, by pointing out that 'you are the tenth one'. This is knowledge from an authority, in this case, the passerby who successfully counts out the ten people. With this knowledge, the counter counts again but this time while including himself. Finally, he comes to realize that 'I am the tenth person' [24].

4.3.5 Arthapatti

Advaita and Mimamsa philosophers employ *Arthapatti* as a valid and independent source of cognition, i.e., as both a *Prama* and *Pramana*. If we break the word, '*Artha*' means a fact, and '*Apatti*' means imagination or *Kalpana*. Together, *Arthapatti* is the supposition of an event to counter contradiction between facts. The Advaita followers employ *Arthapatti* particularly to explain otherwise difficult *Vedantic* texts. While trying to understand the Upanishadic concepts of 'creator *Brahman*', or 'causal *Brahman*', or '*Brahman* as ultimate reality', or theories like '*Jagat Mithya*', or '*Sat Brahman*' or '*Jiva Brahman*', etc. Advaita supposes '*Maya*' as the potential cause connected with all the above.

The *Upanishads* hold that the world is created by *Brahman*. However, *Brahman* does not participate in the creation process of the world, yet *Brahman* is ultimately real. This is a conflicting statement and to resolve this conflict, Advaita supposes that the creation of the world is not the result of any real transformation or *Parinama*, but just an apparent manifestation, '*Vivarta of Brahman*', similar to the appearance of the snake over the rope. Advaita supposes that this manifestation requires *Brahman* to be all-powerful and hence he manifests himself into the world through '*Maya*'.

Arthapatti also means 'assumption'. Advaita uses *Arthapatti* to assume unperceived facts and events which explain the non-congruency in the experienced facts. For example, Advaita employs *Arthapatti* to explain the events of dreamless sleep (*Sushupti*), deep sleep (*Turya*), or pure awareness.

Explanation: In deep sleep, when one does not dream and yet experiences the existence of an objectless consciousness, *Arthapatti* is used to explain the blissful feeling one has after waking up from such a state. Here, the assumption of that 'objectless entity or pure consciousnesses in the deep sleep state is explained by the application of *Arthapatti*.

The usage of *Arthapatti* by *Advaita* is different from that of Mimamsa. Whereas Mimamsa uses *Arthapatti* to resolve conflicts between two facts, Advaita uses *Arthapatti* more as a logical explanatory hypothesis. For them, it is a supposition, an assumption or simply framing (*Kalpana*) of a postulation that explains an inexplicable and unexplainable fact. Dharmaraja Dhvarindra gives the definition of *Arthapatti* as '*upapadya-jnanenopapadika-kalpanamarthapatti*'. This hypothesis in *Advaita* is called '*Upapadaka-Kalpanam*' which is based on the knowledge of a fact called '*Upapadya-Jnanam*'. For example, to explain the empirical fact that Devadutta is fat and does not eat during the day, Advaita through *Arthapatti* presents a hypothesis to explain Devadutta's fatness. Although he skips all daytime meals, the hypothesis is that Devadutta must be a voracious night-time eater. Advaita maintains that their use of *Arthapatti* is only to formulate and explain a hypothesis and not to acquire any new knowledge outside of the presented facts. In that sense, it can be argued that Advaita made the theory of *Arthapatti*, 'consistent'. That is the usage of *Arthapatti* by *Advaita* is to create a framework of explanatory hypothesis based on scientific reasoning, unlike Mimamsa which applies *Arthapatti* as only a source of cognition.

Similar to Mimamsa follower Kumaril Bhatta, Dharmaraja Dhvarindra in his book Vedanta Paribhasa categorizes two types of *Arthapatti*:

1. *Drstarthapatti*, where the assumption is based on what is seen or perceptual cognition.

    For example, a man has two cognitions at two separate moments. First, he sees silver in the seashore. Later, he does not find any silver there. To prove the validity of the second cognition, it is assumed that the first cognition is false, i.e., the man sees an illusion of silver in the seashore. Both cognitions cannot be true at the same time. Hence, the usage of assumption disregards one of the cognitions to explain the other as valid.

2. *Srutarthapatti*, where the postulation is based on what is heard or verbal cognition. It is further divided into two types, namely:
    - *Abhidhananupapatti*: This is a way to postulate the right

words to correct the failure of the speaker who uses wrong grammar in his sentences. In the particular case, where one part of a sentence is explainable and the other is not, it results in syntactical fallacies. Advaita applies *Arthapatti* to postulate another word that fits and corrects the syntax or grammar of the sentence.

For example, the word 'door' in a sentence by itself cannot be intelligibly understood unless it is associated with a state of either being 'closed' or 'open'. Hence a state of either a closed door or an open door is postulated.

- *Abhitithanupapatti*: This is a way to postulate the right meaning to the sentence which has some unidentified facts, even though the sentence is grammatically correct. When the sense of a sentence by the speaker is unintelligible, another sentence is postulated to find meaning to the sentence. This is a postulation to explain the incongruity of meaning in a sentence.

For example, the sentence, 'He is the apple of my eye', is meaningless if the word 'apple' is taken in its primary sense of being an edible fruit. It is only after assuming a contrary or figurative meaning like 'most dear one', that the above statement becomes significant.

The Vedantic version of *Arthapatti* is unique because they apply it to postulate both words and facts depending on the given situation. In that sense, *Arthapatti's* usage by Advaita followers is more flexible and accommodative than the others in explaining a hypothesis and reaching a correct understanding. They employ *Arthapatti* as a distinct *Pramana* that stands on its right to bridge specific gaps in knowledge. Since Advaita believes in all empirical and phenomenal experiences to be relative and finite, their use of *Arthapatti* in postulating an absolute reality stands merit. But *Arthapatti* does not explain the nature of absolute reality, rather shows only a way to understand it. It is an exercise of reason but is not inferential reasoning or perceptive analysis. Besides explaining empirical facts and finite experiences, *Arthapatti* is also used to arrive at philosophical justifications like 'power' or '*Shakti*'. For example, a germ growing into a tree or *Brahman* manifesting itself to the world would be unexplainable (*Anupapanna*), if there were no supposition of Shakti. The world according to Advaita is real in the practical sense but unreal in the ultimate sense. As such, to establish reality as *Brahman*, Advaita uses *Arthapatti* as a very simple process. It is an epistemological instrument to explain their metaphysical claims. It is also an application of reason proper to explain empirical facts and phenomenal experiences. Overall, according to Advaita, *Arthapatti* is a valid and independent *Pramana*.

4.3.6 Anupalabdhi

When we talk about existence and pass judgment on whether an object exists or not, we always rely on facts. A true judgment must always correspond to the fact that provides an affirmation of the existence of an object. A true affirmative judgment for an object's existence always corresponds to a positive fact that has a logical explanation for it. The question at hand is what about establishing the validity of a negative judgment? Are there any negative facts that correspond with it? Most logicians, particularly the followers of Nyaya and the Buddhists, raise the question, how can there be a negative fact, since 'fact', by its very definition, is always a positive statement or event. So, a 'negative fact' is self-contradictory. Negation translates to non-existence. But a fact is an affirmation of existence. So, by that logic, a negative fact also means some form of existence [25]. Three primary questions can be raised regarding the validity of *Anupalabdhi*. They are:

- Can there truly be any negative facts?
- What would be the source of such negative facts?
- What would justify such a negative judgment?

If there is a 'positive' answer to the above questions, then *Arthapatti* can be objectively regarded as valid. In case the answer to these questions is 'negative', it will only be a subjective exploration and nothing more. There are some scholars, who dismiss *Anupalabdhi* simply as nonperception while others see it generally as noncognition. The basic explanation of *Anupalabdhi* as proposed by other schools is that existence and non-existence are two aspects of the same thing and one aspect can be reducible from the other. Hence, there is no need for an independent *Pramana* to specify nonexistence. For example, the condition that there is no jar on the ground (nonexistent) only means the existence of the ground (locus). But Mimamsa school rejects this idea and reports that non-existence and existence are two different aspects and one cannot be reducible to another. Both serve different purposes and both point to different meanings. Advaita, working along the lines of Bhatta, refers to similar ideas at least in the epistemological sense as mentioned in '*Vivarana-Premeya-Samgraha*'. Advaita says that the non-existence of something can neither be known through perception nor inference and there are no other means that can explain the concept. Rather, it can only be known through a unique means of knowledge (*Pramana*) called non-cognition (*Anupalabdhi*) or more specifically appropriate noncognition (*Yogyanupalabdhi*). *Anupalabdhi* is specific to the cause of immediate knowledge of nonexistence which has not been produced by any other source of knowledge [26].

To elaborate further on the understanding regarding *Anupalabdhi*, Advaita says that the existence of an object or thing can be verified by all positive means of knowledge (either perceived, inferred, compared, testified, or postulated). But to know about the non-existence of the same object, which would be immediate and direct knowledge, *Anupalabdhi* is the only means of knowledge. One may question then what all can be known through *Anupalabdhi*. According to Vedanta Paribhasa, four kinds of non-existence can be known through *Anupalabdhi* [27]. They are:

- *Pragabhava*: Non-existence of an effect in its material cause.

For example, a jar cannot be said to be an existing component of its material cause, which is clay, before being shaped into one.

- *Pradhvamsabhava or Dhvamsabhava*: Nonexistence by destruction and annihilation.
- This means the negation or non-existence of a cause that is currently in effect after the production of the latter.
- *Anyonyabhava or* mutual negation: Advaita says by way of a mutual introspection that the negation is found on two objects simultaneously.

For example, a cow is not a horse, and vice-versa. That means the 'horsiness' of a horse is nonexistent in a cow and vice-versa. This explains not only the exclusive difference but also separates the two.

- *Atyantabhava* or absolute non-existence

A particular object, when it does not exist in a particular space frame at a particular time, then it is the case, where the object or thing is non-existent [28]. For example, any form of color is absolutely or totally not present in the sky. Or the evidence for the sighting of a unicorn or UFO is absolutely nonexistent.

A prominent Mimamsa philosopher Prabhakara Mishra never recognized negation or non-existence as a separate category and non-apprehension as an independent *Pramana*. He argued that non-existence cannot be an antithesis and in no way be considered over and above existence, the knowledge of which is known through Perception. So non-apprehension is not non-perception. Further, he argues that no reality corresponds to negation since the reality of any kind is always objective and is experienced in a positive way. As such any negative judgment is only a subjective mode of apprehension [29]. The Buddhists along the same lines and akin to Prabhakara proposed similar views regarding *Anupalabdhi*. The main objections and observations of the Buddhists are:

- Negation or non-apprehension cannot be experienced independently.
- Rather, it is always experienced at a particular time, place, and for a particular object.
- Negation is no real entity because, it by its own virtue, doesn't possess any specific nature that could differentiate it from other positive entities.
- Overall, the concept of negation is feature less and attribute less

For example, when we say 'There is no jar', this only means that we are not able to perceive the jar. It doesn't mean that we see the negation of the jar. The question one can ask is, 'What is then the negation of the jar?' The Buddhists in their assertions conclude that the absence of an object is inferred from non-perception of that very object, which is a no-sense-object contact. Non-perception is self-luminous because the statement 'There is no jar on the ground' simply means that the jar cannot be apprehended at the desired place and this in turn asserts the locus that is the ground.

Advaita holds negation or non-existence's *Pramanyata* as primary along with the existence or presence of something. Non-apprehension is a distinct *Pramana* as perception or inference. However, the problem of negation is still a matter of debate that persists even today. While the early Advaita followers inquired about 'How to know negation', the latter emphasized 'What is negation' [30]. However, both the Bhatta philosophers and the Advaita followers, the primary defendants of *Anupalabdhi*, agree that negation cannot be perceived without any 'sense-object-contact'. So, this makes it impossible to be known through perception. Negation cannot also be inferred without the availability of *Vyapti* or the invariable concomitance that becomes the reason for inference. So, it is not an inference. Negation cannot also be known through testimony in the absence of any verbal cognition. Similarly, it cannot be also explained or known through comparison or *Arthapatti*. It is only fair and right to come to the logical conclusion to call negation an independent category that can be known through an independent *Pramana* called non-apprehension or *Anupalabdhi* [31].

4.4 Comparative Analysis

Knowledge is the foundation upon which our practical activities in relation to any particular object depend. But knowledge is not always the correct representation of reality and hence knowledge for various reasons can be valid or invalid. According to Dharmotra, the eighth century CE Buddhist scholar, valid knowledge or *Prama* is the knowledge of a previously unknown object (*Anadhigata-Visayam-Pramanam*) [32]. This new knowledge must be free from error or doubt and should not be a memory or recollection. Besides, this knowledge must be non-contradictory (*Avisamvadaka*) [33]. Here non-contradiction means that the knowledge must be presented in such a way that it fulfills the practical needs of that very object. The knowledge must be about the object and also lead to its revelation. Thus, it can be said that the Buddhist conception of knowledge is pragmatic in nature.

Advaita Vedanta also proposes a theory of noncontradiction (*Abadhitatva*) [34]. Advaita argues that a purpose can be fulfilled even if it is based upon a false cognition. For example, an object glowing at a distance mistaken for a jewel can turn out to be a jewel even if the initial cognition that 'it is a jewel' is based on a false belief [35]. This may happen due to various reasons but the point is that the purpose is fulfilled. Besides non-contradiction, Advaita also considers 'novelty' as another important characteristic of *Prama*. Thus, its definition of *Prama* or Valid knowledge is a cognition in which the object is neither contradicted nor previously known as the object (*Anadhigata-Badhitartha-Visayam Jnanam*) [36].

A *Pramana* is an active and unique *Karana* (cause) of *Prama* or Knowledge. In this regard, there are many causes necessary for the production of knowledge. But common to all is the 'mind' which is a necessary condition for all kinds of knowledge. We have already discussed that Buddhists only accept two types of *Pramana*, *Pratyaksha,* and *Anumana*. They either reject or reduce the other type of *Pramana* to the above two. But Advaita accepts all six sources of knowledge as independent *Pramana*.

Amongst all the *Pramana*, knowledge gained through *Pratyaksha* is considered the most reliable and valid cognition per se. But there is a difference of opinion regarding the nature of perception. Perception can be either *Nirvikalpa* (indeterminate) or *Savikalpa* (determinate). *Nirvikalpa Pratyaksha* is the immediate apprehension or the bare awareness or the direct sense-based experience that is undifferentiated and non-discriminative [37]. In general, the Buddhists hold that *Pratyaksha* is always *Nirvikalpa Jnana* and indeterminate in nature.

According to Dignaga, *Pratyaksha* is indeterminate in nature because it is pure awareness that cannot be conceptualized in thought. Concepts are formed in the mind but perception is driven by the object and hence, is not the product of the mind [38]. Dignaga quotes one expression from the *Abhidharma* treatise citing examples: the term *'Nilam Vijanati'*. The expression means one perceives something as blue but cannot express it because it signifies the immediate awareness of the object, i.e., the color blue. Only when the person associates the color blue with an object, he can express so.

Early Advaita followers, similar to the Buddhists, believed in only *Nirvikalpa Pratyaksha*. They understand reality to be of the nature of pure existence which is devoid of any characteristics. And all things are only imposed on the truth (*Nirvisesa Sanmatram*). Any determination requires discrimination by *Buddhi* and qualification by an attribute. But the core Advaita philosophy that 'the world is an illusion' or '*Jagat Mithya*', rejects any qualification by the mind.

The neo-Advaita followers, however, accept a distinction between *Nirvikalpa* and *Savikalpa Jnana*, but from the *Vyavaharika* or practical standpoint. *Savikalpa Pratyaksha* is the knowledge of an object qualified by an attribute. In essence, it is the determination of an object by means of predication or assertion. Knowledge of an object is gained through the lens of its specific characteristics and involves predicting and asserting certain aspects of the object based on the observed qualities. This process gives uniqueness to an object and accounts for its identification. *Nirvikalpa* is the bare existence of a thing that does not require any predication. For example, '*Tattvamasi*', or 'you are it' is directly perceivable and hence *Nirvikalpa*.

Although the Buddhists consider inference a valid source of knowledge, its relevance is secondary to that of perception, while trying to understand reality. We have previously discussed in this chapter that the Buddhists employ greater emphasis on direct experiential awareness and encourage personal self-realization through meditative and mindful practices. An inference or Anumana is often used in Buddhism as a supportive tool to aid in direct insight. It is used in the pragmatic context to support the understanding and practice of the core Buddhist principles.

The Advaita followers utilize *Anumana* as a significant tool for understanding the nature of reality, interpreting scriptures, and harmonizing with direct experiences. It holds a central position among the valid means of knowledge to establish the non-dual nature of reality along with the identity of the individual self (*Atman*) with the ultimate reality (*Brahman*). Inference is utilized to render a deeper meaning to the primary texts. The Advaita masters in the past have used inference to strengthen their own arguments and subsequently defeat opposing philosophical views. But like the Zen Buddhists, Advaita followers also focus more on direct experiences through self-inquiry.

The emphasis in Buddhism has always been on direct perception and the means of achieving it. In this regard, the concept of *Upamana* or comparison is not a matter of central focus in Buddhist epistemology. Rather it is only employed as a valuable means of conveying the teachings and facilitating an in-depth understanding of the *Sutras*. The Buddha himself used analogies, similes, and metaphors to illustrate tough concepts and guide his disciples. Comparison only serves as an expedient means to help the *Buddhists* understand difficult concepts about their faith, employed skillfully by the masters. Comparative analysis is an important tool for communicating and teaching, but the concept is not deemed as an independent source of knowledge like it is in Advaita Vedanta.

Advaita considers *Upamana* or comparison as a valid means of knowledge or *Pramana*. The use of *Upamana* is particularly relevant in explaining the metaphysical doctrines. This understanding is important in the early phase of the aspirant's spiritual journey leading up to self-realization. By applying appropriate analogies, the master can deliver his teachings in a familiar language through which the disciple can understand the message comfortably. It serves as a stepping stone aiding the metaphysical truths. Some thinkers have objected to giving

Upamana an independent *Pramana* status. Amongst them, some dismissed it as a case of *Pratyaksha* while others called it to be the case of *Anumana*. But Advaita taps the various applications of *Upamana* as an explanatory tool that has its usability while relating the unknown, simplifying non-dualistic principles overcoming the limitations and provisional nature of language, and aiding in spiritual practice. Advaita employment of *Upamana* is to bridge the gap between the known and the unknown. Their advocacy of *Upamana* as an independent source is so strong that they also have a theory regarding the knowledge of dissimilarity [39]. According to this theory, knowledge regarding dissimilarity is also obtained through *Upamana*. It is applied to understand that, there is complete dissimilarity between the phenomenal world qualified by a *Saguna Ishvara* and absolute reality unqualified (*Nirguna Brahman*), yet this distinction is not real. The world is not real but only a manifestation of *Brahman*.

The Buddhists do not consider verbal testimony (*Shabda*) as an independent *Pramana* whereas Advaita does. They maintain that the intent of the speaker is implicit in the statement and can be understood from it. To validate the information, the hearer must independently verify the facts that are heard. When one hears any words, the intent of the speaker can be inferred by the hearer after establishing the trustworthiness of the speaker. So, *Shabda* is basically inference. But Advaita not only recognizes *Shabda* as an independent source but also accords a higher place of importance in the list of *Pramana*. Their explanation is that there are certain facts, which can be supposed by authority alone, like the concept of a '*Nirguna Brahman*'. Advaita believes in an entity without any attribute called *Brahman* as the highest authority and that this fact is only a self-revelation caused by *Brahman* itself. As one progresses in his spiritual journey, this truth about *Brahman* truth becomes self-evident. So, one needs only to believe in the tradition and faith in the scriptures.

But to a rational mind, understanding is supposed to be free from the appeal of any form of testimony both divine and secular. Authority is recognized in religion but in philosophical and logical investigations, only immediate sources of direct perception and inferential reasoning are accepted as valid sources of knowledge, as in Buddhism [40].

There is a prolonged controversy about the relationship of *Arthapatti* with *Anumana*. In *Arthapatti*, one starts from the knowledge of a known fact to a presumed fact, in order to resolve any conflict. Through *Anumana*, one starts with the cognition of one thing and ends with a different cognition. But in *Arthapatti*, one starts with an unexplained fact and arrives at the explanation of the same fact [41]. In Advaita Vedanta, *Anumana* is employed to analyze the external world and its workings, aiding the explanation of cause and effect. But Arthapatti is used to explain certain situations from the Vedas and Upanishads, where direct evidence is not provided.

Advaita goes the farthest in defending and subsequently assigning independent *Pramanyata* to *Arthapatti*. Generally, it uses this method to interpret complex Vedantic texts. But more specifically, Advaita employs it as a method to suppose unperceived facts and principles, and, use the new information to explain experienced facts [42]. Their use of *Arthapatti* is to overcome any insufficiency or contradiction arising in other means of knowledge. For example, one may find some contradiction in some perceived or inferred facts. Then, one may apply *Arthapatti*, to postulate another condition to solve it.

For the Buddhists, non-apprehension or *Anupalabdhi* can never be experienced independently. It is spatiotemporal in nature and pertains to a particular object. Negation is not a real entity because it does not have any specific nature of its own and lacks any real character (*Abhaba*). The absence of something is not known through negation but by the position of a particular thing [43]. Something which cannot be apprehended in a particular place, only confirms the presence of the locus (*Adhisthana*). For example, the book is not present on the table only confirms the absence of the book in that particular position and that becomes the basis for inferring that the jar might be in another location which is the locus. The absence of an object in an expected place is the confirmation of the existence of the same thing in a different place.

But Advaita differs from the Buddhists, by assigning independent status to *Anupalabdhi* as the sixth valid source of knowledge. *Anupalabdhi* is valid because it reveals a specific type of knowledge about non-existence (*Abhaba*) which cannot be known through any other *Pramana*. According to Parthasarathi Misra, in his book Sastradipika, everything has two distinct forms, existence, and non-existence [44]. For a particular object, its own existence is real. But equally real is the nonexistence of all other things in that object. Since they are two very separate properties, they are mutually irreducible. Advaita concludes that the non-existence of something cannot be known through perception or inference, but through a unique means of knowledge called non-cognition, more specifically through appropriate noncognition (*Yogyanupalabdhi*).

According to Madhusudana Sarasvati in his book Avaita-siddi, *Yogyata* means that the non-existence of a thing in a certain place is appropriate, and the existence in that place is opposed to its nonperception [45]. This means *Yogyata* or appropriateness is the position, where all the conditions for perceiving an object are favorably present, yet the object is not perceived. It means, that a condition where something could potentially be perceived is not experienced in real-time perception. Examples of *Yogyatanupalabdhi* are optical illusions, selective attention, hidden or partially hidden things, inattention, etc.

However, Zen Buddhism and Advaita Vedanta when compared through the epistemological lens, offer different ways of knowing through their unique approaches owing to developments in distinct cultural and philosophical settings. But there is also the profound revelation that both traditions offer diverse yet converging paths for the understanding of reality and the true nature of knowledge. Zen advocates 'directly pointing at the mind', in order to transcend the limitations of language and intellectual understanding. It offers meditation and direct experience as the means to deconstruct habitual dualistic thinking. All theories about knowledge are part of the dualistic thought process. The aim of Zen is to break away from all constructs and experience the unfiltered version of existence which is true reality.

Comparatively, Advaita Vedanta relies on the wisdom of the Upanishads and employs all possible means for rightfully interpreting the message for the benefit of the individual. Zen Buddhism advocates for a direct experience of the self. Similarly, Advaita Vedanta employs the method of self-inquiry or *Atmavichara* to realize the ultimate unity of the self and *Brahman*. The inquiry is aimed at breaking the barriers of the illusion of an external world and then coming to an ultimate realization of the nondual nature of existence. The common message of both traditions is that underlying our sensory world there lies a true version of reality. The truth about that reality is necessarily revealed through a direct experience and this is the key to transcending the limitations of ordinary thinking which is a world of multiplicity based on dualistic thinking. Truth cannot be found out by intellectualization but is only revealed through intuition.

References

1. *Buddhist Epistemology* by S.R.Bhatt & Anu Mehrotra, Greenwood Press, 2000, Page 4348
2. *Ibid, Page 26*
3. *Ibid, Page 27, 29*
4. *Ibid, Page 29*
5. *Ibid, Page 30*
6. *Ibid Page 58*
7. *Ibid, Page-67 8. Ibid, Page-68 9. Ibid, Page-76*
10. *Ibid, Page-71*
11. *Vedanta Paribhasa, vide D.M Dutta, The Six Ways of Knowing, Page-24*
12. *Bijan Biswas, Pratyaksha Pramana in Advaita Vedanta, Indian Philosophical Quarterly, Vol. XIV, No. 1, January-March,1987*
13. *A Critical Study of Indian Philosophy, Chandradhar*

Sharma, Page-197

14. The Six Ways of Knowing, D.M Dutta, Page173
15. Ibid, Page-174 16. Ibid, Page-176 17. Ibid, Page-181 18. Ibid, Page-132 19. Ibid, Page-209
20. Ibid, Page-283
21. Authority in Indian Philosophy, by S.K Sinha, Philosophy East and West, Vol. 1, No. 3 (October-1951)
22. The Six Ways of Knowing, D.M Dutta, Page- 286
23. Authority in Indian Philosophy, by S.K Sinha, Philosophy East and West, Vol. 1, No. 3 (October-1951)
24. Panchadasi by Vidyaranya, vide D.M Dutta, The Six Ways of Knowing, Page-295
25. Arthapatti: A Critical and Comparative Study of the Views of Purva Mimansa, Advaita Vedanta and Nyaya-Vaisesika System, G.Pratap Simha, Sri Venkateswara Press, 1991
26. Shikamani and Maniprabha in Vedanta Paribhasa vide D.M Dutta, The Six Ways of Knowing, Page-155-156
27. Ibid, Page- 146
28. Vedanta Paribhasa, vide D.M Dutta, The Six Ways of Knowing, Page-151
29. Ibid, Page- 338
30. Ibid, Page- 356
31. A Critical Study of Indian Philosophy, Chandradhar Sharma, Page- 224
32. The basic ways of knowing, Govardhan P. Bhatt, Page-78 (original source- Nyayabindutika of Dharmottara)

33. Ibid-Page-78
34. The Six Ways of Knowing, Page-19
35. (Tattava-pradipika-citsukhi), vide D.M Dutta, The Six Ways of Knowing, Page-19
36. Vedanta Paribhasa, vide D.M Dutta, The Six Ways of Knowing, Page- 24
37. A Critical Study of Indian Philosophy, Chandradhar Sharma, Page-194
38. Buddhist Epistemology by S.R.Bhatt & Anu Mehrotra, Greenwood Press, 2000, Page -39
39. Paribhasaprakasika by M.M Ananta Krsna Sastri, vide D.M Dutta, The Six Ways of Knowing, Page- 131
40. Authority in Indian Philosophy, by S.K Sinha, Philosophy East and West, Vol. 1, No. 3 (October-1951)
41. The basic ways of knowing, Govardhan P. Bhatt, Page- 330
42. The Six Ways of Knowing, D.M Dutta, Page- 206
43. The basic ways of knowing, Govardhan P. Bhatt, Page-341
44. The Six Ways of Knowing, D.M Dutta, Page- 137
45. The Six Ways of Knowing, D.M Dutta, Page- 142

Chapter 5
Ethics and Morality

5.0 Introduction

If metaphysics is the exploration of the fundamental nature of reality and epistemology is the investigation into the nature of knowledge, then ethics in philosophy is the bridge that connects the metaphysical aspiration with epistemic expression. In other words, ethics is a condition for guiding all actions that one ought to perform within our reality. While performing actions, knowledge is gained in the process about self and the world. Such knowledge isn't only about the action but also about the considerations made while performing such action.

Ethics is the bedrock upon which relationships are built and societies are maintained. It is considered the foundation for the moral grounding of an individual. What a man does with what he knows, is the gist of an ethical consideration. So much so that, in its absence, a society may potentially lead to chaos and conflict revealing the worst in men. According to T.P. Kasulis, in any cultural setting from which ethics and morality evolve, there can only be two philosophic orientations, namely the intimacy setting and the integrity setting. The former setting sets the ground for a responsive action towards a moral context. While the latter sets about a responsible reaction to the moral context. Integrity matters when one needs to assign the relationship between one's self and others in an extraneous condition [1]. This is a developed ethical response between two separate entities based on the situation, which suggests that any ethical content is not inherent in man, and man only acts according to his surroundings. With the help of certain external values, principles, and virtues, man shapes his response to others, out of necessity and not because of any inherent nature. It is the idea that dominates Zen, that is to think of others, particularly the sentient beings not as objects of morality with whom we have preconceived or inherent moral adjustments, rather the focus is on the just treatment, as per situation and necessity.

In the presence of the setting of intimacy, morality is defined by internal conditioning [2]. It is the conditioning that there is an inherent moral obligation towards others brought about by internal conditioning and not external necessity. Unlike the integrity setting where new links are developed and the code of morality assigned, in the intimacy setting morality is assumed. Zen is a mix of both of the settings, where moral principles are developed according to the cultural setting it is in.

Buddhism mostly evolved as an opposition to the traditional Hindu social value system practiced in ancient India. But elsewhere, particularly in China, Buddhism developed in association with little continuing opposition from the Confucian and Taoist value systems prevalent in ancient China. So, ethics in Zen is a mixture of social settings based upon intimacy and integrity, and its moral and ethical content evolved over the years, sometimes totally reinvigorating itself, yet remaining true to the original teachings of Sakyamuni.

According to Radhakrishnan, if the ethical apparatus can be assigned to anyone in this cosmos, it is the individual, who is both the subject and the locus of ethics and morality. The highest 'good' or goal one can achieve according to Advaita Vedanta is 'self-realization'. Anything else that leads a person to fulfillment of 'self-desire' and away from self-realization is 'bad' [3]. This 'good' according to Advaita Vedanta is spiritual wisdom and self-knowledge which should be preferable over sensuous satisfaction and ego gratification. Until one attends self-realization, he is bound by the consequences of his actions whether moral or immoral. All activities whether *Manasika* (mental), *Vacika* (verbal), and *Kayika* (physical), irrespective of appearing as noble or altruistic, are insufficient for man to achieve the moral 'goodness' because he has not yet realized his true self. This man is bound to suffer because all these activities are rooted in self-desire. A man must transform and redirect his activities towards attaining self-realization. Only then can his activities be truly called 'good', according to Advaita. Any activity, desire, or thought that leads man along the path of realization is morally justified. The traditional Indian approach is that the means justify the end. It's the intentions that matter and not the result. But in Advaita Vedanta, the end does justify the means provided that the end is the highest value, i.e. 'self-realization'.

Anything a man does, after he has attained the highest good of 'self-realization', is justified and morally acceptable according to the Advaita. The realized person can neither be a judge himself nor be judged by anyone from the phenomenal world. His actions can no longer be measured on the phenomenal scale of values. This man or realized sage understands that he is truly non-different from others as non-different as he is from the 'one'. The Advaita followers understand this positive expression as 'love'. Love for one own 'self'', love for the self in 'others', and the overall love for everything 'else' as a part and parcel of the one true reality, Brahman. The Advaita masters emphasize taking the path of knowledge. But to do so, out of love is the highest possible 'virtue' one can cultivate to reach the highest 'value' of self-realization.

In this chapter, we analyze the ethical contents of

5.1 Ethics in Zen Buddhism

Buddhism promotes not only individual awakening but also the liberating potential in all sentient beings. On a much larger prospect, Buddhism stands strong on the idea of all-encompassing compassion for all beings, both living and nonliving. If we trace back to the initial message of the Buddha, he said that his teaching was the only way to understand life which is *Duhkha*. And then reveals the way to end *Duhkha*. Following the footsteps of the Buddha, the early Buddhists understood the end of suffering to be in the attainment of *Nirvana*. But *Nirvana* is not a migration or refusal in a different dimension of reality that transcends the current one. It is not also just the ability to see the immanent nature of reality through an experience of overcoming all physiological barriers like passion and creed. The traditional understanding of Buddhism is 'transcendence' which is a process of escaping this world full of suffering. The physiological understanding is that of 'immanence', to see the world as it is without being involved. But a deeper understanding of Buddhism as it is in Zen, is transformative, i.e. about a real transformation of the self rather than just 'self-adjustment' in this world.

Zen as an ethical and moral prospect of transformative Buddhism, opposes the devaluing of *Samsara*, and with it the idea of shunning birth into it forever. It also argues against finding a mindful adaptation of a distinct position of the self in the same world. But what it really promotes is a novel way of realization, where the 'experiencing world' and the 'individual experience' are neither real nor unreal, but only constructs, that can be experientially deconstructed and reconstructed by following the path of the Buddha [4].

That being said, the Zen masters caution their disciples to maintain ethical conduct and follow the Buddhist precepts [5]. Such practice is necessary to prolong the concentration of the mind. But they should in no way be established as a means to awakening. Zen still adheres to the moral code of conduct set by Buddhist ideals, yet for its uniqueness, Zen does it differently than other Buddhist schools. There is no defined ethical system of philosophy in Zen, but it does not imply that Zen lacks any moral content. Over time, Zen masters have shown extreme moral courage and determination, self-discipline, and true empathy and compassion for all living beings.

According to one Chan Buddhist master Yun-qi Zhu-hong in the 16th Century CE, the mind in essence is neither good nor evil per se. It is rather an instrument to contain the evil and project the good. All acts first emerge as thoughts in the mind. Zen masters affirm the original five precepts that have been practiced since the time of the Buddha. Such practices lay the groundwork to cultivate the power of the mind. Its function is to concur the evil lurking, so very eager to express itself through man, and in its place project and practice good thoughts and deeds. The five precepts are:

1. Non-killing or abstaining from taking any life
2. Non-stealing or abstaining from taking what is not given
3. Abstaining from sexual misconduct
4. No lying or refraining from false speech
5. Refraining from intoxicants that cloud the mind.
6. The mind through which enlightenment is expressed

is also the source of morality. And enlightenment as such requires preconditioned moral actions that lead to the former [6]. On one hand, an astute sense of morality is a condition for enlightenment, on the other, an enlightened person, who is the bearer of the Buddha nature and Buddha mind itself, becomes a natural at performing morally just actions with a cohesive sense of justifying Buddhahood in others. The enlightened one performs actions without any ethical judgment or reflection and without any preference or condition. This is because the 'awakened one' or the 'enlightened man' acts out of an absolutistic and non-dual standpoint that emerges from deep within. In such a state, that person is impervious to any external stimuli, yet balanced in his response to any sensual inquiry. The balancing is between the impulses that he receives through his senses interacting with stimuli, and his actions in response to the external data received and processed in the mind. He remains unaffected in all conditions.

This innate sense of morality is unprovoked in a layperson but fully activated and functioning in the enlightened one. The Zen way of understanding what constitutes good or bad is based on a clear-cut distinction between what is considered moral or ethical. The argument made by scholars like Douglas A. Fox and A.D. Brear is that for an enlightened one, morality comes naturally and supersedes any claim over an action by society in terms of being ethical or not [7]. That being said, the enlightened one acts without any hesitation or calculation and without any differentiation or identification. A moral person is by default an ethical person. But the tag, 'ethical action' becomes irrelevant to an enlightened one, because his innate and continuous sense of morality, i.e. his Buddha mind, sees through all actions without any attachment or motivation. Unlike an ethical act, which requires the adherence to certain standards set externally through social expectations, a moral person, such as in Zen, performs because it is Buddha - nature that reveals itself. So, any act performed by him is neither hasty nor considered but is spontaneous and yet is according to how the Buddha would have conducted himself.

In terms of an ethical philosophic system, the Mahayana concept of the Bodhisattva ideal is very much preferred and practiced in Zen. The Bodhisattva is an accomplished Buddhist, more so than anyone else, in showcasing cohesion of true wisdom and pure compassion, through his actions. His workstation is the *Samsara*. His goal is to walk his path through the *Samsara* into the revealing of *Nirvana*. Samsara is both a necessity as well as a condition for finding *Nirvana*. A Bodhisattva is not defined by what he is supposed to do, but by what he does, which is anyway exactly what he is supposed to do. But not according to the norms set by society but by the strength of the Buddha innate in himself, who works through him, showcasing a balanced and undifferentiated act.

Any sense of morality or ethics as a prescription is shunned by Zen. Moral conduct is descriptive in Zen, inasmuch that a morally apt act is what an enlightened person does, naturally on account of his Buddha nature. For such a person, wisdom is his mental state, which he continuously is aware of. And compassion is the expression that emerges out of the Bodhisattva, through his actions [8]. But the Bodhisattva before he becomes one, is a normal person, who with a certain kind of interest pursues a specific spiritual journey.

Traditional Buddhists bind themselves to certain rules and take certain vows, which are based on the moral and ethical standards set to attune to social expectations. Vows are made to maintain benchmarks set in the spiritual journey by the enthusiasts. Fulfillment of such vows is nonnegotiable but for certain exceptions. Vows are conditioned standards set externally that constrain the freedom of the oath taker to act independently. And Zen does not oppose the following of precepts and maintaining of vows, because, in the initial state, one needs continuous motivation and enthusiasm both from within and externally, to transform from being 'just someone' to becoming the 'awakened one'. It promotes and encourages to live according to certain standards and conditions, with the view that true harmony is in practice. And all efforts should be made, including living by the code and leading by conduct to achieve perfection in 'practice'.

The concept of self-realization is both the metaphysical goal as well as the ethical standard that the Zen practitioner follows to attain enlightenment. The idea of enlightenment in Zen is to become like the Buddha and adopt his nature as one's own. But in the process, the Zen follower commits to cultivating a well-defined set of virtues, values, and moral sense that changes his thoughts and actions from a confined, restricted, and biased way of looking at things to a natural, free-flowing, and spontaneous way [9]. It is this spontaneity that the Buddha had, which is also there within everyone according to Zen. This innate desire to do good needs only to be initiated in man. Upon initiation, one becomes the embodiment of good. One attuned to the Buddha nature. Everyone's original nature is the Buddha nature, and the eventual goal is also to realize the Buddha nature.

It is the 'potential Buddha' or *'Bodhisattva'* in oneself that leads one to be a Buddha.

Although there is not a defined ethical system in Zen, a practitioner lives a very ethical life. A life led with an iron will to cultivate a particular way of meditation to achieve self-realization and an unbreakable oath to see the Buddha nature in all sentient beings and help them in their needs. Primary among the ways a Zen follower commits himself is to cultivate the practice of Zazen (meditation upon the self). The practice of Zazen involves a journey of realization with the external support of masters, rituals, routines, and codes, moving along the inward and intuitive path of self-introspection. The presence of specified moralities, virtues, and the insatiable desire to attain perfection in practice, helps fortify the mind, which is the apparatus through which the Zen practitioner will attain realization.

To a Zen practitioner, nothing is more important than the code and conduct to continuously strive for perfection in the meditation practice. Zen monasteries or schools may differ according to region or geography, but one thing that is common and confirmed in every Zen institute, academy, and organization is a specified hall dedicated to meditation. The regular practice of sitting and meditating (Zazen) or the act of just sitting silently (*Shikantaza*), highlights the importance of meditation in Zen. The main aim of such facilities is to condition the mind into practicing meditation rigorously to prepare him to receive higher knowledge. Yet, paradoxically, Zen also claims that enlightenment cannot be achieved by hard and conditioned work alone [10]. Zen masters warn that one may maximize one's effort in practicing meditation by going through extreme hardships and toiling, yet one may not achieve enlightenment. One does not become Buddha by imitating him, but by realizing his innate Buddhahood, and acting spontaneously and naturally without biased conditioning and interests.

No expert can authorize enlightenment. That is to say that, any act done based on merit is still a biased action, and no amount of goodness accumulated in the process can lead to enlightenment. Realization happens through an earnest inquiry of the self, and enlightenment comes from within. Hence, one can condition oneself to vigorous practice, but one may still not achieve perfection just by practice. For certain philosophical explanations, Zen does turn to scriptures or language. Zen prefers to see beyond the principality centered on concepts, or the logic and reasoning set to justify those concepts. Zen also sees the empirical investigations done through analysis of language as unnecessary, and conforming to social demands and expectations as meaningless, if the goal is to reach enlightenment. True enlightenment is projected from the self and no amount of confirmation or validation can make one attain enlightenment because true enlightenment is the recognition of the self by the self.

The most comprehensive understanding of morality in Zen is done about enlightenment. Both enlightenment and morality are the same [11]. There is no enlightenment without having developed a strong and unbiased sense of morality. But just being a moral person without having truly achieved enlightenment is incomplete. Morality as a virtue can be cultivated at any stage of life, but it is also not impossible to find someone who does not need any outward motivation to be morally just. There will always be some, who have a natural tendency for performing morally correct actions, without being conscious or calculative about it. This capacity for good from a very early age in some people is the justification for karma.

According to Zen scholar Ichikawa Hahugen, karma is located in the doctrine of innate Buddha nature [12]. Different people vary differently through their exertion and accumulation of power and wealth, maintaining of certain status and health, and even being born as a specific gender. All social connotations in context to a particular man, are a form of retributive justice on account of his past Karma depending on whether he was good or bad in his previous life. Social differences, between being rich or poor, privileged or deprived are accepted justifications for karma. The retributive effects of karma are a way to reveal and justify the social differences that a man is subjected to in society. It is a way for him to accept that he was born to a certain way of life because of a certain reason.

But the innate Buddha nature that is the common identity in all sentient beings, unites all men with the shining ray of hope that one can annihilate all his accumulated karma if only one can recognize the Buddha that dwells within. This idea promotes the 'equality in difference' point of view [13]. Amidst the different social conventions, and made-up identities that we so dearly cling to, we share a sense of equality because of the Buddha nature that is deeply seeded within us.

While looking at the historical evolution of Zen, some scholars argue that while Zen does offer a unique approach to enlightenment, it lacks a moral dimension in its practice, where morality and ethics do not occupy the central stage [14]. A Zen follower approaches *Satori* or enlightenment while being a morally just person, but his intentions are not contained in an explicit display of practice and advocacy of moral and ethical behavior. Zen enlightenment does not bear any particular significance on the moral character of man. A Zen practitioner trains to attain the state of 'no-mind' (*Mu-shin*), which is the primordial condition of the mind before it attracts and associates itself with conscious thinking about something. He suffers in his mind while being trained to do an exhaustive deconstruction of his experience of the world by continuously affirming and negating all that he experiences until he finds himself in a state of eternal peace within himself when he is no longer bothered by the dualities and modalities of the world. He finds himself completely unsettled by paradoxical analyses and thus remains less than enthusiastic to reflect upon the moral dimensions of his personality.

A Zen practitioner does not strive to achieve moral excellence, yet the inclusion of an early sense of morality without reflecting too much on it is the Zen way. On achieving *Satori*, he does not show any eagerness to give any moral output to society because it is expected of him. He acts without any constraints, expectations, or discrimination. He acts intuitively out of the Buddha nature that he realizes within himself. He acts out of spontaneity and not reflection [15]. The state of enlightenment which he strides for, is achieved after conquering the mind. A conquered mind according to Zen, does not require the stamp of morality or reflection. This is because, a Zen mind is characterized by vast emptiness, clarity of openness, and unapologetic nonattachment to all things. A Zen mind is trained as such, that it is free from distractions, preconceptions, and ego drives and is not stamped as 'moral'. The cultivation of awareness is the primary goal of Zen. Having attained that, the Zen practitioner can apply the new sense in his daily life by fostering an honest sense of compassion without speculating too much on it. Being also a Buddhist, he is expected to live by expanding his sense of kindness and responsibility towards others. But nothing is more important to him than the attainment of 'total awareness' or the cultivation of 'mindfulness'. This is the practice of arriving at a stage where one becomes aware of each moment without ever indulging in it. After attaining *Satori*, the world does not become different, but one does see the world differently. Not by any polarized viewpoint of reality or with any standard set of morality, not by the ethical expectations of society, or by the proud achievement of his individuality, but by emphasizing the importance of living harmoniously with himself and with his surroundings.

The contrasting ideas that a Zen practitioner is innately perfect and yet can use a little improvement, both hold true [16]. He is ever in danger of clinging to the one-sided view of perfection. Upon realizing the 'emptiness', he can get attached to the idea and not see it for what really it is. The Zen masters ask their disciples to have an open mind while in their pursuit. The idea is to open the mind as much as possible, and strike it with relentless paradoxical questioning, until the mind becomes impervious to any form of speculation and condition it is subjected to. So, to say that a Zen practitioner is perfect is to say that he has an astute sense of morality already implicit in him, at his innermost core (*Tathagatagarbha*), ready to reveal itself. Yet, he can still improve tremendously through Zen by cultivating an ideal Buddhist state of mind, through compassion and emancipation. But his goal should not be to become the epitome of morality or to set standards for ethics. Rather all his energy should be spent on attaining a 'direct experience and understanding' of all things, without identifying them as things. The aim is to cultivate the mind, to limit thoughts to a single-minded focus, by seeing through the duality, and thus clearing the illusion.

5.2 Ethics in Advaita Vedanta

Advaita Vedanta is a philosophic system of nonduality that was formalized into a school by Adi Shankaracharya in the 8th century CE. It's one of the most successful philosophic schools in India and continued to flourish through subsequent masters by direct transmission from the teacher to the disciple. Masters like Mandana Misra, Vacaspati Misra, and Padmapada were instrumental in formalizing the earlier commentaries of Shankara along with their veneration of the primary scriptures. Its emphasis was on the unity of the soul (*Atman*) with the Paramatman (*Brahman*). However, it might be observed that ethics has not been given a separate treatment as much as metaphysics and epistemology because of Advaita followers' unwillingness to assign a separate dualistic status or a distinction of individual soul when the entire focus is to unify with the absolute. Ethics is somehow, assumed in Advaita Vedanta, for it is the very foundation of self-inquiry.

Man is innately unable to understand unity amidst diversity [17]. The cause for the world is *Brahman*, but man, unable to see through the difference, gets convinced that the *Visesa* (the contents of diversity or the world) are distinct or *Bhinna* from *Brahman*. Although it is a simple process to be able to see through the *Bheda* (distinction) for unity, it is not easy. It will require strong moral foundations and true ethical content in a man. The stronger the value system that the man can develop within himself, the clearer his path will be. Shankara asserts that the path of true enlightenment is revealed only to that individual who has purified his mind and body, continuously and rigorously. He needs to be positioned to receive higher knowledge for which he must have vehemently observed the *Yama and Niyama*. These are the ethical faculties that define the character of an individual, such as *Ahimsa* (non-violence), *Satya* (truthfulness), *Astreya* (Abstinence), *Brahmacharya* (celibacy), *Aparigraha* (Non-attachment to possessions). Although the *Yama* and *Niyama* are popularized primarily in the Yoga Sutras of Patanjali, there are other *Yama* mentioned elsewhere in the Upanishads. In *Sandilya* Upanishad, there is mention of *Yama* like *Dhrti* (fortitude), Arjava (sincerity), *Ksama* (forgiving), *Mitahara* (balanced diet). There is also mention of *Niyama* like *Santosha* (contentment), *Tapas* (austerity), *Svadhyaya* (studying texts), and *Ishvara Pranidhana* (Godliness). Shankara was aware of the need for a disciplined life to observe the life of a truth seeker. Certain rituals and mantra rites, help in preparing the individual during his journey. It helps to focus the mind and strengthen self-inquiry.

But their relevance should be reoriented in the advanced stage. For the Sannyasins, who were desirous of *Moksha*, Shankara was very particular about the virtues that they reflected in their daily lives expressed through their actions [18]. Such virtues as highlighted in the Bhagwat Gita as *Udasina* (indifference and unbiased), *Adambhitvam* (modesty), *Saucam* (purity), *Acarya-Upasana* (serving the needy), *Ahimsa* (nonviolence), *Atma-Vinigraha* (self-control), *Anahamkara* (submission), *Samacittata* (Equanimeous), and (*Ananya-Yogena Bhakti Avyabhicarini* (unyielding devotion to the supreme). When such virtues are practiced with true penance over some time, it will reach its maturity. And that's when wisdom will dawn in.

The understanding of a non-dual nature of reality brings a uniqueness to the ethical aspect of Shankara's Advaita. According to him, the true veneration of the sacred scriptures, the very source of Advaita ethics is based on *Dharma*. Man is obligated to the fulfillment of his dharma in two spheres of his life. One that should reflect in his actions (karma known as *Pravrtti-Dharma*) and the other defined by his insatiable quest for *Jnana* (knowledge or *Nivrtti-Dharma*) [19]. *PravrttiDharma* is fulfilled through adherence to one's *Varnashrama* and *Nivrtti-Dharma* is fulfilled through self-purification or *Sattva-Suddhi*. This very notion, act, and achievement of karma and *Jnana* form the base for the ethical ideals in Advaita.

Man's karma or his *Pravrtti Dharma* or simply karma yoga according to Advaita is an otherwise indirect path to *Moksha* [20]. When the *Dharma* is under siege, and *Adharma* reigns, because man falls prey to his *Kama* (unchecked desires) and *Aviveka* (non-discrimination between the good and bad), the Lord descends through an incarnation or *Avatara* on earth to uphold *Dharma* and vanquish *Adharma*. But on the part of man, by focusing on his karma while observing his *Dharma*, Shankara says, man can attain *Moksha*. But such a path is only an indirect means to *Moksha*. It should be observed with detachment and absolute devotion to God (*Ishvara*). With persistence, man can rid himself of *Rajas* and *Tamas* and attain *Sattva-Suddhi* or self-purification. Only when man proves his competency to walk the path of *Jnana Marga*, he can attain so in due time. His actions or karma, in his lifetime, the ones he is in control of, are an indirect means to realize the supreme which is the same as attaining *Moksha*. As stated in the Gita, a detached action is a pure and sinless action that protects man and advances him in his pursuit [21].

According to Shankara, *Moksha* or *Mukti* is the state where one receives knowledge through intuition, and all sense of identity and belonging becomes meaningless in a state of eternal consciousness. Such a state though very much possible in this world, yet for all the worldly duties and distractions that man thinks he has, they lose their individual status and particular worth, once he attains *Moksha*. It is a state of *Sarva-VyavaharaAbhava* or absolute *Niskarmya* (detachment) [22].

There is still an identity consciousness, where a *Mukta* or liberated being is seen as an individual doing particular work. But to him, he is not a detached soul but a realized soul, and that convinces him of being the same as Brahman. In such a state, worldly affairs do not affect the *Mukta*, because he engages in them dispassionately. Hence the condition of practicing *Dharma* or *Adharma* does not apply to such a man. *Dharma* is necessary and holds valid in the phenomenal world. But in the enlightened state, when *Jnana* dawns, all *Dharma* and *Adharma* transcend to the *Parmarthika Avastha* (Absolute Bliss) [23]. Such a state is possible by abstaining and refraining from all worldly affairs and dedicating life to total contemplation on Brahman. According to Shankara, this is *NivrttiDharma* which consists of the relentless pursuit of *Atma-Vidya* or knowledge of the self and then subsequently relinquishing all activities. With *Pravrtti-Dharma*, one will accumulate merit and cut his sin, but once ready and with the accumulation of *Nivritti-Dharma*, all concepts of merit and sin disappear and all that remains is the sublime realization of bliss.

The scriptures serve as the foundational inspiration to serve the lord the right way, in adherence to Sanatana *Dharma*. But Shankara says that the contents in the scriptures only affect the *Vyavaharika* realm, i.e. in this world. Man is deeply affected by *Avidya* and in effect tends to dissociate himself from his true nature by associating with false identifications. It gives him a false sense of satisfaction (*Preyas*), which is still deeply rooted in Avidya. Shankara lays great emphasis on the Upanishadic *Mahavakya* 'Tat Tvam Asi' (that you are), which according to Shankara, is the simultaneous dissociation and association that man undergoes, dissociation with all his earthly possessions and association with the ultimate. So Vedic knowledge can prepare man, train him, and help him maintain his strength and purity up to a certain extent. But the ones who seek *Atma Jnana*, must at once abandon the Vedic ways of rites and rituals, injunctions and prohibitions, and all those activities that involve worldly affairs and promise earthly merits. The purpose of *Atma-Jnana* is not to attain a high seat in *Svarga* (heaven), nor to enjoy being the best version of oneself on earth, but to transcend all concepts of heaven and earth. The purpose is to reach a state of absolute consciousness, where a heaven on earth or an earthly heaven does not mean anything insofar as they all mean the same.

Man is an embodiment of Brahman, in flesh and blood. Since man is born with a definite purpose and for a limited time, he is bound by certain *Upadhi*. Man becomes a man by the action he performs, and any action by man is because of his limiting *Upadhi*, the primary ones of which are his senses, his mind, and his body. These are the only instruments that man possesses, through which he can justify his time on earth. Man's reliance on his body, mind, and senses for his actions makes up for the *Vyavaharika* realm, of which man is a part and parcel. It is only the appearance of the *Parmarthika* or the Brahman, through man's limiting *Upadhi* that he sees himself and others as individual souls that gives the false impression of external souls. Based on this distinction and identification, a man sets the ground for the ethical module that he creates to govern his life with a specific code. But these codes are necessary for man to see through his ignorance. The Advaita firmly believes that it was initially Brahman who emerged in the world of men with limiting faculties. And man became aware of this fact through his *Upadhi* or limited ability. But it is the same *Upadhi* that sprouts the inquisitiveness in man to trace back his origin. And by mastering his *Upadhi*, he completes his journey and reaches the truth.

So, to be a man is to perform actions, and to act is to use the limiting ability (*Upadhi*) that he possesses. His ability is limited because it caters only to the *Vyavaharika* or relative realm. Hence all his actions, whether ethical or unethical or whether performed from a sense of morality only matter in the phenomenal world. As long as man identifies the self with the body, he will be subjected to morality. But once he realizes that the true self is not the body, nor the mind, but the same as the all-pervading Brahman, he no longer remains limited by his *Upadhi*. This is to say that he no longer is bound by any sense of morality and ethics nor can he be judged based on any standard.

Perhaps the single greatest emphasis as laid by Shankara and subsequent Advaita followers is on the *Jnana Marga*, for he affirms that Jnana is the only true and immediate means to Moksha [24]. Shankara helms this *Marga* as the cardinal principle in following Advaita. But *Jnana* according to him, is not the attainment of some knowledge that leads one to the ultimate goal. Rather it is the highest state of experience through which it is possible to transcend the empirical world. It is an experience of Brahman or *Brahma-*

Saksatkara [25]. The transcendence according to Shankara marks the path for *Mukti* or *Moksha*, where all thoughts and actions concerned with the *Vyavaharika* and marked by *Avidya* and *Ajnana* are abandoned for the experience of *Parmarthika* marked by the attainment of *Jnana* or *Vidya*. A true Advaitin is expected to rise above the lies and deceit of the very convincing waking state and transcendent into bliss (*Ananda*) through his *Siddha*. Only through *Jnana*, is it possible to attain *Mukti* (*Jnanad eva Kaivalyam*) [26]. *Moksha* according to Shankara, the primary *Purusartha* that can only be achieved through *Jnana* alone.

This accretion by Shankara does not mean, he is opinionated regarding man's status of being evil in this world, rather man is only governed by *Avidya*, and because of *Avidya*, man is subjected to the conditions of good and evil. And *Avidya* can be annihilated only by acquiring *Jnana* or true experience. With such an experience, all concepts that define man in terms of good, bad, and other conditions of morality cease to hold any worth on man. This transcendence of man, says Shankara is to abandon all sense of self-hood and embrace the ultimate sense of selflessness. Self-hood is assigned by a man to himself and others because of his actions, which man is bound to. But *Mukti* or *Moksha* is a state of rest and tranquility. So, *Jnana* and not karma will lead to the latter. But karma is the necessary predisposition for *Jnana* to dawn in.

Purification of mind and body is possible only through karma but karma alone is insufficient for a direct realization. Karma only prepares one to receive higher knowledge. When karma is perfected with diligence and persistence and later renounced (*Sarva-karma-Sannyasa*) without being attached, the body becomes the right vessel to receive ultimate wisdom.

The act of renunciation after having acquired the perfect conditions for the body and mind, is the highest form of action that a man can perform. Such an act is possible only on the part of one who is a *Stitha-Prajna* or the one with steady or consistent wisdom [27]. A *Stitha-Prajna* is steady and in control of all his thoughts (*Stita-Dhi*). He is in a continuous state of ecstasy through all his actions (*Samadhi-Sta*) and is an embodiment of a truly enlightened person (*Vipascit*). *Stitha-Prajna* is the content of *Jivan-Mukti*. A *Jivan Mukta*, or liberated one, becomes so on account of his *Stitha-Prajna* but a *Stitha-Prajna* is a man, who has covered substantial ground in his pursuit of spiritual fulfillment. And with *Sthithata* (consistency), he will be well ahead in his quest. A *Stitha-Prajna* dwells in the pursuit of *Pratyagatam* or introspection of the self and renounces even the most fundamental and compelling desires that make him a man, like progeny and sensual gratification. His sole delight is in the study of the self [28]. He is equally unaffected by both the favorable and unfavorable circumstances. That is to say that he has full control over his mind and no attachment to his body. He is also vigilant against his senses which will always be trying to seduce him by attacking his discriminating power (*Viveka*) into submission and inefficacy. This underpowering of *Viveka* gives power to *Bija* or germinating power and man engulfs himself in the fire of unending and unyielding desires and provocations.

Unlike the *Jivanmukta*, a *Stitha-Prajna* is still a struggler, who continuously keeps his senses and his response to his senses in check and on alert. He is a man of profound insight who is more advanced than most others in the pursuit of knowledge. And when he becomes a *Jivanmukta*, he lives only with the bare necessities required for living. By abstaining from worldly activities, he initiates the process of burning all his karma. And this subsequently refrains him from accumulating further karma. His body which is an effect of his *Prarabdha-karma* will be fully seen lasting till all the karma *Phala* (fruits) is reaped. The *Mukta* without then being attached to the world, himself, and others becomes the bearer for *Loka-Yamaha* or the collective good of all people. All his actions then will be spontaneous and according to all standards of morality and ethical correctness, but without himself ever partaking or being bothered by the assessment. The path to enlightenment is an intense solo *Siddhi*, but after its attainment, and as long as the body is alive, the Mukta works for the good of all the people and dedicates his remaining life to the service of the needy and vulnerable. Although there is nothing more that he desires to achieve in the light of the ultimate fulfillment, yet, he continuously acts and strives for more but only for the betterment of others. From the perspective of a *Mukta*, however illusive the world may be or howsoever ignorant man can become, he still leaves real incentive for the world and its inhabitants that reflects in his actions.

This is an act without any personal interest for the *Mukta* and is only an incentivized action for the uninitiated. This is called *Niskama karma*. [29]. To offer a theory that the world is illusory is not to infer that it is unreal. Advaita ethics does encourage one to live a detached life, where the pursuit of vested interests should be insofar that they are purposive and help one progress in his spiritual journey. This detachment does not imply total rejection of the world, but rather it asks people to take a non-attached approach towards everything. This will eventually bring peace and equanimity to the person with a detached outlook. Non-attachment also means to perform a selfless action. A detached action strengthens a feeling of selflessness in the individual. And this invokes a divine urge in him to work for the welfare of others. Continuous use of *Niskama karma* or a detached action, unworried about results, yet doing it to the best of one's ability, with the available resources at hand, only helps the Advaita follower to move closer to realization.

The necessity for one to be moral is a predisposition before the sprouting of *Jnana* in man can happen [30]. *Jnana* as dictated by Shankara is the ultimate means of *Moksha*, but karma is required before *Jnana* can be attained. But then karma is useful till Jnana dawns in. This does not mean that in the presence of *Jnana*, karma vanishes.

It does not serve further purpose to the *Jnani*. So, his is then a life defined by sacrifice, which allows him to serve even though he is not obligated to offer any service to anyone anymore. He does not serve his needs anymore but rather offers his remaining life in service of others. His actions are then performed out of a sense of duty and dedication to Isvara (*Isvara-Samarpana-Buddhya*) [31]. To Shankara, the fulfillment of one's duty is the true offering to Ishvara, for worship of *Ishvara* lies in the service of others. While serving others, one needs to do so with total detachment or *Asangatvam*.

Shankara's *Ishvara* is a soul cleaner and its worship helps in the attainment of *Buddhi-yoga* [32] which is a highly advanced stage of absolute control of *Antha-karana* or the internal senses, developed out of intense spiritual engagement through devotion. But true devotion according to Shankara is a detached worship of *Ishvara* performed not in expectation of any rewards, but out of *Sva-Dharma*. All action even that of devotion should be performed with spiritual discipline in the light of spiritual experience.

Shankaracharya through his Advaita only reveals his theory of illusion of the world but he does not emphasize it because of the possibility of a higher understanding that man can attain. This understanding, Shankara says is that of *Jnana*. But *Jnana* cannot originate in man without his karma. So, man with his limited *Upadhi* is also powered by *Viveka*, with which he segregates his karma and directs all his thoughts and actions to Brahman.

Advaita Vedanta encourages the use of the rational faculty or *Viveka* (discrimination) more so than any other mental faculty. It is not an idealistic philosophy asking its believers not to engage in *Karma Yoga*. It is realistic because it does not ask its followers to follow its teachings blindly. Rather it encourages one to approach Brahman through reason. Shankara asks for the study of the scriptures, the practice of austerity, engaging in dialogues, and yet to fulfill one's social duties, duties towards family, self, and others. Amidst all this, he also cautions, that reason can take someone only so far. At one point in the journey, one has to abandon reason for intuition to be ready to receive higher knowledge. So, it is only reasonable to discriminate between the essential and the unessential, between real and the unreal.

Exercising the discrimination faculty (*Viveka*), more and more, helps one to lead a more meaningful life than others.

In Shankara's Advaita, *Jnana* holds as the direct *Marga* to enlightenment and helps one realize the true meaning of Advaita. Why the *Jnani* is then concerned about the *Jagat* which is devoid of any value, and is only a mere illusion? Any concern about the *Jagat* and its dwellers is then only an emotional attachment aimed at the welfare of people. But morality is part of the *VyavaharikaVyavastha*, which is governed by *Avidya*. So, there is no point in attaching any value to this illusive reality. For an enlightened way of life, says Shankara, no morality or virtues can be attached or associated [33]. An enlightened person is not obligated to anyone else. Yet, the enlightened one cannot refrain from action, since the illusion persists. The enlightened one slowly retires to inaction or *Naiskarmyan* or *Naiskarmya-LaksanaSiddhih*), but while doing so, he works for the betterment of others, not out of any social responsibility because the material conditions cannot be changed for others. It is not a collective outcome that the illusion gets unveiled from the truth. Rather it is a strict subjective journey, in the sense that man accepts the inequalities that govern the society, but yet remains detached from it, unaffected by the outcome of his actions. It is because in enlightenment, the only thing that can remain is good, and hence, any act the enlightened one performs is intuitively good. The act may be retiring into inaction, or completely engaging in the service of others, indifference remains the only value.

5.3 Comparative Analysis

Early Buddhist ideals had more in common with Advaita Vedanta than any other heterodox schools of Indian philosophy. Particularly, the case of morality was seen through the lens of a practicing set of codes, principles, and values that aimed at personal liberation as the highest goal. The aim of the Buddhist system was for man to free himself of the *Duhkha* of the *Samsara*. Along similar lines, the aim of the Brahminic system was for man to free himself from the subsequent cycles of death and rebirths which are hugely set by one's karma that plants the seeds for experiences in the future.

Morality was seen as an internal component for individuals to acquire the liberating truth or *Jnana* according to the Advaita Vedanta. The moral content in man was assumed, because only in the context of purity in character and clarity in conduct can *Jnana* originate that leads him further to being a *Mukta*. All Indian systems except the Charvakas regarded morality and knowledge to be the two sides of the same coin, intertwined and interdependent.

But as we discussed previously in this chapter, Zen unlike most other forms of Buddhism and other schools from its place of origin, rejects ethical and moral conditioning as necessary parts for the journey of awakening [34]. Zen also does not preassign the contents of morality and ethical behavior. The sole purpose of Zen is to be able to focus and eventually perfect the act of meditation. But this does not mean that Zen does not give any importance to ethics or sees itself as beyond morality. Only the priority of meditation over the precepts and ethical constructs finds prominence in Zen [35]. But ethics is not altogether rejected in Zen. The practice of Zazen, reveals the Buddha nature within man. Similarly, the practice of ethical codes and conduct as set by the monastery and teachers actualizes and authenticates the Buddha nature by strengthening the feelings that reflect on the daily actions. The adherence to ethical code and moral setting is the affirmation of the Buddha nature which highlights how the awakened one acts. It is the ultimate expression of the Buddha's nature that does not compel one to be good but assures that he is good.

In Zen, emphasis is certainly laid on trusting the masters and old ways, but the ultimate authority over what is right or wrong rests in self-experience. Master Dogen laid more emphasis on the monastic codes than the precepts [36]. According to him the upholding of moral guidelines is not a process of self-purification but is the ultimate Buddha nature that one innately has, lying in the dormant stage, itching to be unleashed. For Zen, a moral code is not prescriptive, but merely descriptive, because moral correctness is the ultimate Buddha expression that surfaces itself in man from man. Other teachers like Eisai, emphasized strict adherence to Buddhist precepts and monastic guidelines. Adhering to the precepts mentioned in Fanwang-jing and following the monastic guidelines as dictated in the Dharmaguptaka Vinaya was strictly observed in the Rinzai Zen schools. This suggests the flexibility regarding the moral codes and ethical conduct as part of Zen's way of life. Morality is necessary but not absolute in the path to awakening. It helps in Zen awakening but is not a prerequisite for achieving so.

According to Advaita Vedanta however, a sense of morality is necessary and the most preferred way of dwelling in the *Vyavaharika* realm, and in the cycle of Samsara [37]. But all assigned values for morality get lapsed for a realized soul. In Zen, the awakened one acts intuitively according to the Buddha nature ever so dwelling within him. Similarly, a *Mukta* acts out of dispassion and nondiscrimination of the good from the bad. For him, the only act that he can perform is good, because in enlightenment only good persists. When the enlightened one, because he acquires true knowledge, is freed from *Avidya*, then no act can be morally assigned to him, nor can he be judged on ethical grounds. This is because morality and ethics only matter in the *Vyavaharika* which is governed by *Avidya*. With the dissolution of *Avidya*, all evil is vanquished. Hence, any act that has evil in it, is a psychological impossibility for the *Mukta* [38].

The only reason one should be moral in his life is because through its path man becomes able to strengthen his character and purify his soul otherwise infested with sin. He is also able to deepen his insight further so that eventually it leads him to salvation. In short, creating a morally just atmosphere generates a favorable frame of mind, ready to receive higher knowledge through the ultimate experience of realization. In the process, meditation only helps the aspirant with further insight. But it is not the ultimate goal, i.e. to become the best at meditation. The final goal is still the attainment of enlightenment. Truth is ever positioned at the center and surrounding it is a veil of false dispositions and injections. A developed sense of morality and ethics uncovers each layer like a peeled onion until all that remains is the truth.

The knowledge of the self must be cultivated from within the self, for the truth is innately embedded in the self. Shastras and sutras do not compel man to be moral or ethical. But their existence is only a reminder of what can be collectively achieved if people can develop an astute sense of morally just and acceptable behavior for one another. Man is innately divine, and the contents of divinity are love and compassion. These are the greatest virtues that one can cultivate. The feeling can then be extended to others, not out of any desire for moral perfection or ethical justification nor because he stands as an embodiment of justice, but for his innate nature, that attracts him, to all of creation out of love, compassion, and a clear sense of unity.

References

1. Zen as a Social Ethics of Responsiveness, T.P. Kasulis, Page-8
2. Ibid, Page-10-11
3. Advaita Vedanta- A Philosophical Reconstruction, Eliot Deutsch, Page-99
4. A New Buddhist Path: Enlightenment, Evolution, and Ethics in the Modern World, David R Loy, Page-40
5. Is there a Zen Ethics, James Whitehill, Page- 14
6. The Nature and Status of Moral Behavior in Zen Buddhist Tradition, A.D.Brear, Philosophy East and West (Oct-1974), via- James Whitehill,
7. Is there a Zen Ethics, James Whitehill, Page- 22-23
8. Ibid, Page-24
9. Ibid, Page-25
10. Ibid, Page-28
11. Invoking Reality: Moral and Ethical Teachings of Zen, John Daido Lori, Page- 1
12. The Oxford Handbook of Buddhist Ethics, edited by Daniel Cozort and James Mark Shields, Page-235
13. Ibid, Page- 236
14. Satori and Moral Dimension of Enlightenment, Dale S. Wright, 2006, Page-3
15. Ibid, Page-10
16. A New Buddhist Path: Enlightenment, Evolution, and Ethics in the Modern World, David R Loy, Page-133
17. Religion and Ethics in Advaita, Jacob Kattackal, Page-153
18. Ibid, Page-246
19. Ibid, Page-212
20. Ibid, Page-213

21. *Bhagavad Gita, Vide Religion and Ethics in Advaita, Jacob Kattackal, Page-214*
22. *Ibid, Page-214 23. Ibid, Page-215*
24. *Ibid, Page-219*
25. *Ibid, Page-219-220 26. Ibid, Page-220*
27. *Ibid, Page-226-227*
28. *Ibid, Page-227 29. Ibid, Page-223*
30. *Ibid, Page-236*
31. *Ibid, Page-236-237*
32. *Ibid, Page-240*
33. *Ibid, Page-241*
34. *The Oxford Handbook of Buddhist Ethics, edited by Daniel Cozort and James Mark Shields, Page-221*
35. *Ibid, Page-225*
36. *Ibid, Page-226*
37. *Indian Philosophy, Vol-2, S. Radhakrishnan, Page-578*
38. *Ibid, Page-579*

Chapter 6

Aesthetics

6.0 Introduction

The principal motif of all philosophical investigation in Buddhism is the persistent effort to dissolve the duality between the experiencer and the experienced by breaking down the barriers that separate both in terms of subject and object, or the self and the external world. By questioning the constructs of reality, which is the total of our experience, man comes to a much deeper understanding. True reality is 'not dual' but 'non-dual'. All Buddhists strive for transcendence. In Zen, transcending the limitations and all thoughts ordinary by applying methods of disciplined meditation and rigorous contemplation is enlightenment. It is both the spiritual aspiration as well as practical expectation in Zen, i.e. to be able to perceive non-duality.

A non-dual state replaces all differences and distinctions that bound man, with a sense of unity that liberates him. The experience of reality as a variable change of events and perceptions is replaced by the understanding of constant change. In the ordinary thinking process, reality is constantly changing and uncertain. But to be able to experience non-duality is to be able to embrace and acknowledge the constancy of change itself. Rather than doubting the variable nature of reality, man embraces the idea that change is an inherent and unchanging axiom of existence. So, any psychological discontentment is replaced by spiritual fulfillment.

If non-duality is the only true state, then perusing it is the only true good. And all things good are beautiful. So, in a journey like this, an astute sense of beauty or aesthetic clarity is born, which is the central point of this chapter. In a much contemplative sense, to view something aesthetically means to be able to really 'see' the beauty in a thing and not just merely 'look at' it and call it beautiful. It is the same thing as submerging one's thoughts and feelings into an object so that an individual's subjective identity becomes intertwined with that object or experience. And this makes the object identifiable and the experience relatable. This consummation between the self and the other is achieved through subjective investigation but without any objective reference. One cannot practically merge the 'I' and the 'IT', but can do so in his mind, by expanding consciousness and attaining awareness. Both of these, in the Buddhist sense, are the actual contents of true beauty. To tap into the infinite potential of consciousness and to be able to do so while being fully aware or present in each moment, is to be able to see the beautiful in all things, without being affected by it.

Arthur Waley suggests that the depiction of Zen to most people who have some knowledge of it is that of a 'Far Eastern Art' [1]. He further writes that art was often regarded as a form of Zen, because of the Buddha features that everything innately carries within itself. If we consider Buddha to be the most beautiful and his ways to be utterly graceful, then to carry that nature in ourselves, and to be able to recognize this hidden form, is nothing less than an art, revealed by the carrier's determination, just like a painter, bringing life to an abstraction through his commitment.

However, Zen art never really flourished for a prolonged period in China as it did in Japan. The Japanese understood Zen, more so with the aesthetic experience, finding its practicality in daily activities. To a Zen artist, a painting may be an attempt to practice the dissolution of identity, or the surrendering of his self, where he may see himself in the painting as the same as the landscapes, birds, animals, and flowers, which he paints. This the artist does to invoke his inner Buddha and reveal its nature duly. Other forms of art may include painting of life episodes of the Zen masters. The true intention of Zen art is to reveal Buddha nature and Zen firmly believes that this Buddha nature is present in all of nature, both sentient and non-sentient beings. So, art inspired by nature is very intimate to the Zen follower [2]. Besides, highlighting the Buddha nature, the purpose of art in Zen was also to find beauty in the mundane. For example, a menial activity like serving tea, called Chanoyu or Sado (The Way of Tea) is conducted very attentively and involves a very elaborate ceremony. The purpose of this serious execution of a rather casual activity is to draw out a person from his self-related concerns which otherwise consume him. And allow him to heighten his sense experiences, and realize the interconnectedness and harmony in all things surrounding him. Zen practitioners claim that if one can see the harmony and the interconnectedness of all things through a simple activity like serving tea, one can also experience the non-dual totality, through the same activity [3].

Through the study of the beauty and pleasure associated with fine arts like architecture, poetry, and music. Advaita in a limited capacity, strives to have a sensual grasp and gratification of the absolute. The purpose of art is that of delight, as an immediate effect. Apart from immediate pleasure, art is also intended to give a totality of experience, by making room for aesthetic contemplation [4]. The aesthetic contemplation greatly affects the aesthetic value or rasa, or the essence of the art that implies that true appreciation of art is a continuous process, of which sensory satisfaction is only the immediate effect. However, it does not last for long, and dissipates away, bringing about a new form in its place. The totality of experience is in terms of a dispassionate interest in the art and further insight into the art, to understand that, which has not been communicated directly by the artist, and that which remains hidden under the surface message intended for its viewers. By analyzing art deeply, its situation, its surface value, and its hidden message, one may hope to get a glimpse of the absolute or taste of the ultimate experience. This is the gist of aesthetic investigation in Advaita Vedanta.

In Advaita Vedanta, *Rasa*, or *Rasa-Anubhav*, is the most contributing factor in the study of the beautiful and pleasure. *Rasa-Anubhav* or the aesthetic experience is attainable at two levels, that of the *Paramarthika* and the *Vyavaharika* [5]. At the *Paramarthika*, it is the experience of *Ananda* from the realization of Brahman--Atman. *Ananda* is not the effect of Brahman's realization, but it is Brahman's realization itself. So, in the absolute, the aesthetic experience is that of *Ananda*, or absolute bliss, attained through realization.

At the *Vyavaharika*, *Rasa*-Anubhav is that of pure joy which is but diluted by karma because they are the byproducts of *Avidya*, which reins strong in the *Vyavaharika*[6]. Even with *Avidya* persisting strong, one can still have a glimpse of the absolute, or the taste of the *Ananda*, in a very limited capacity. *Avidya* is still reigning strong, but its contents and karma are under temporary suspension, because of the influence of extraneous situations. Art plays a very dominant role in providing this experience and hence, both the art and the artist are held in very high regard in the Indian milieu like Advaita. Through art one can vaguely but briefly grasp the mystic and the transcendental.

6.1 Aesthetics in Zen Buddhism

There has never been an independent branch of learning called Buddhist aesthetics. However, the aesthetic richness in the classical Buddhist works cannot be ignored, and hence a study into this aspect and into the Buddhist thought and way of life can be warranted. Buddhism is primarily known for its integrated yet unique form of Eastern spirituality that adapted itself into the local culture, wherever it spread and evolved as a cultural celebration of infused ideas. In China, where the idea of Zen further developed, Buddhism absorbed the essence of Chinese Confucianism and Taoism, and the blueprint of Zen was conceived. With a revamped philosophy, Zen also introduced a uniqueness in its practice. Its impact on the culture is profound, especially its contribution to the arts [7].

Unlike other religions, the preamble in Buddhism emphasizes the process of creation rather than the creator. Buddha was not a creator per se, but rather a man who achieved enlightenment. His life was the perfect example of confirming the central idea in Buddhism that every human can become a Buddha because man is innately qualified. This is why, Buddha serves as the primary inspiration and guide for every Buddhist. The values adopted by the Buddha emphasized the reality of life situations. He taught the truth about suffering, the meaning of compassion, and the way to inner peace. The evolution of the Buddhist thought process through these three interconnected yet distinct doctrines, implies that there is a transition in Buddhism from ethics into aesthetics in its study of metaphysics. Initial Buddhist teachings emphasized heavily ethical conduct such as the eight noble paths, to guide individuals to live a morally justifying life that will lead to *Nirvana*. However, the search for metaphysical inquiries in Zen is a result of a fusion of ethical principles and the perception of beauty.

The exploration of impermanence and interconnectedness needs a contemplation of the beauty that is inherent in the natural order of things to be grasped fully.

In a philosophical sense, Buddhist aesthetics is the commonality of 'pleasure' that is felt in comprehending its doctrines and theories. It's about finding the ultimate sense of appreciation, tranquility, and joy in the teachings of the Buddha, symbols representing them, and practices that are correct according to the Buddha. The concept of finding inner peace, which is the end goal in Buddhism, is nothing but the attainment of aesthetic pleasure in its true sense [8]. So even though there was no specific learning of aesthetics in Buddhism as in the West, the aesthetic laws of virtue in terms of Buddhism cannot be overlooked. One idea so prolific in Buddhism is that outer beauty is only a manifestation of the inner [9]. The central issue in Buddhism is that of dualism: its identification, understanding, and overcoming concerning man, the opposition between life and death, and the skepticism between one's self and the other that make all the problems in life. The solution is to reach a state of 'non-dual entirety' while maintaining an undifferentiated attitude throughout. Meanwhile, the Buddhist standard upon which the nature of beauty is defined falls under the study of aesthetics. For example, in the Buddhist sense, a beautiful craft, although non-sentient, can be defined as something that is in peace because it aspires to be so [10]. Similarly, a Bodhisattva is someone, who has transcended himself beyond the realm of duality. And in this transcendence, there is beauty, because beauty in the true Buddhist sense is liberation and free from duality.

But the idea of beauty cannot be contained by the self, or restricted by the other. It is to say that true beauty cannot be a point of view, since all points of view are mere assimilation of the dualistic thought processes, which the Buddhist wants to free himself from. To assign a status of not beautiful or ugly is to do so relatively. But to the Buddhists, true beauty is not in opposition or confirmation. It presupposes both the ideas [11]. The realm of true beauty is the one that is unsegregated and without the conflict between what is beautiful and what is ugly, which cannot exist or be realized other than in the non-dual state, or the Buddha realm.

To become a Buddha, one cannot do so using the distinction between a lower self and a higher self, but to have no distinction at all. It means that the self and the Buddha are one. Buddha, cannot be objectified, rather it can be realized when the distinction between the subject and object is annihilated. The word '*Soku*' which is used in Japanese Zen, closely represents this idea of annihilation of distinction. It is a direct connective or an immediate and bare identification of the affirmation with the negation without any distinction.

Along similar lines, another Japanese word that contributes to the Buddhist worldview is the '*Fosoku furi*', which in English can be loosely translated as simultaneously being unattached and undetached at the same time. This state represents the infinite potentiality that can be achieved by being fully aware of the present. This represents the deepest sense of beauty, which cannot be found merely in the explanatory or descriptive. Deep in the Buddhist thought process, there is the fact that extremely beautiful objects have some elements of irregularity in them. They are perfect the way they are, because of the distortion or uncanniness in the view, which adds a uniqueness to the artifact. True beauty is in the dissolution of the sense of beautiful and ugly amidst the distinction which present at all times. One has to see through the distinction to see beauty in its reality.

The spirit of Zen aesthetics is not imbibed in the value appreciation or sensual gratification, rather simplistically and humbly, it aims to help experience beauty in daily life, doing mundane chores, and yet not just watching it but working at it too [12]. The idea of beauty according to Zen, is not a static sense, where things are appreciated in their final form. Rather, it is a dynamic flow of all things, and the ability to see the beauty in chaos. Besides, Zen also champions the idea that there is beauty in poverty. Here poverty may not only be understood in terms of wealth accumulation, but the exploration of the idea that the greatest of achievements have the humblest of beginnings. In context to Zen, it means true beauty can be found in the simplest of objects, unpretentious, and easily relatable. The most beautiful objects, particularly art, are the ones that do not exhibit a final statement about themselves, rather suggesting the idea that true beauty that is represented by a particular form, is much more than what meets the eye.

Zen aesthetics, particularly in the Japanese tradition, is more focused on the very acceptance of the notion of impermanence [13]. The concept as introduced in Zen aesthesis is called 'Wabi-Sabi'. In English, it roughly means the presence of an eternal beauty that is present in the things that are not perfect, transient, and incomplete. It also explains that the idea of beauty is imbibed in the process and not found in the final form. The emphasis is on paying attention to the details, which are often overlooked for the final product. There is a certain steadiness in experiencing the beautiful, because, the process is given more emphasis rather than the form. And this happens over some time. Unlike the Western standards for beauty, which are often represented by something grandiose, Zen promotes the idea that true beauty is in the small things and hidden meanings. It is the subtle aspects and temporary phases, which are often overlooked by the conditioned eye. True beauty comes with age, which in the life of an object is greatly molded by the notion of impermanence (*Mujyou*). If only one can understand that nothing lasts forever, and everything is always in the process of creation, one can then understand that nothing is ever perfect, and all things are perfect the way they are. One needs only to realize it. This is Wabi-Sabi, and the true definition of beauty [14].

According to Zen, a sense of beauty is truly born with the dissolution of dualities, particularly the dissolution of the subject (I) with the object (it) [15]. This is possible only when non-duality is understood in its entirety. In a more philosophic sense, true beauty can only be experienced, not by seeing one or the other, but by knowing one's true nature (*Kensho*). It is a Japanese word associated with Zen, where *Ken* means to see and *Sho* means nature. So, to an artist who is true to his art, there is no distinction between his form and his audience. To him, the form is the same as the person watching it, and the person watching it can appreciate the art for what it truly is. The perception of beauty becomes clear only after one abandons the self. This is the price of admission.

In the chapters relating to metaphysics and epistemology, we discussed the advocacy of intuitive knowledge, or *Paramarthika* truth over inferential knowledge, or *Samvritti* truth by the Buddhists. In context to Zen, the faculty of intuition is paramount, in understanding beauty because the intuitive faculty in man, allows the individual to look directly at the object, just like it allows the individual to look directly into one's nature [16]. The impact of this faculty is limited when viewed conditionally and relatively. To utilize this faculty to the fullest, one must leave it with free flow, and allow it to run its course with unrestricted supervision. It means to attain knowledge of non-duality where the standard of beauty is not in assignment or distinguished but is in unity and recognition of things as they are. Intuition is the power that fuels this awareness and allows one to see things as they are.

The idea of beauty and pattern are synonymous to one another [17]. Particularly concerned with arts, the creation of a pattern and identifying it as beautiful is the same thing, from a human perspective. The best experience of an object is when it is done so, intuitively which is impossible for the vulgar eye, but made possible after realization. Our intellect is conditioned to view an object in parts so that our mind can comprehend it. But through intuition, the object can be viewed in its entirety, insofar that it gives insight, directly into the object's essential nature. To be able to recreate this experience within the human mind is to be able to create a pattern, and by nature, it is beautiful [18]. It is not the pattern assigned for particular objects, but an overall pattern to see everything with a non-dual attitude.

The world according to the Buddhists is born out of love which also represents our primordial home. And that is the realm of true beauty. This love signifies that there is a certain interconnectedness and interdependence in all things that make up the external world. This love is also a binding force that fosters a sense of unity and compassion for all things, sentient and non-sentient. The idea that this is also our primordial home as well as the realm of beauty is nothing but the confirmation that true beauty is in the achievement of enlightenment. And only after one acknowledges his suffering, can he attain enlightenment. It is a journey of transcendence from suffering to awakening. There is a beauty in this transition. The Buddha represents both the worlds of suffering and awakening which are eternally beautiful. Hence, there is a craving in man to see this beauty, since both worlds represent the Buddha dwelling within all of us.

6.2 Aesthetics in Advaita Vedanta

When we say aesthetics in the Indian context, it means the scientific and philosophic study of Indian fine arts [19]. But unlike in the Western sense, the scope of fine arts in Indian philosophy has always been that form of expression that presents the absolute, in such a way that it can be sensually grasped or at least comprehended in a limited capacity with the gratifying feeling of inner satisfaction. In that sense, only three forms of art, are recognized as independent forms and have been primarily philosophized upon, namely architecture, music, and poetry. The philosophic views of these three art forms according to Indian authorities are known as *Vastu-Brahma Vada* for architecture, Nada-Brahma Vada for music, and Rasa-Brahma Vada for poetry.

The major developments in Indian aesthetics are roughly said to have been advanced in seven hundred years. The earliest available works in any Indian art form existing today can be credited to Bharata's dramaturgy (*Natya Shastra*) around 500 CE. A philosophic text of architecture available today is the Samarangana Sutradhara compiled by King Bhoja of Dhara in the 10th-11th century CE. Subsequently, the first existing work on the philosophy of music was compiled as Sangita Ratnakara by King Sarnga Deva around the 12th to 13th century CE.

The word art in Sanskrit means *Kala* which is defined as an activity that is pleasurable to an individual or humans in general. It involves a series of calculated steps or moves defined by a keen sense of observation and a clear display of expression [20]. All this is physically perfected while continuously contemplating upon the art form, to justify its use, secure its mastery, and fulfill its ultimate goal of experiencing the absolute. For the practitioner, art provides an objective platform to get a satisfying experience of the absolute, limited only by the prevailing subjective conditions of the experience. This is to say, that the more potential a practitioner of fine arts taps into, the more satisfying his experience would be of the absolute.

According to the Indian aestheticians, poetry (*Rasa-Brahma Vada*) is considered the richest and greatest among the three art forms. The art form of drama (*Natya*) is considered the most accomplished form of poetry. Dramatic representation according to Indian aestheticians serves as the best medium to showcase the various situations that affect life. Drama, a form of both pictorial and musical representation for a particular case, appeals both to the listener and the looker. In a more philosophic sense, the three aspects that make up the drama, namely, the dramatist or the director, the actors, and the spectators, offer three different points of view of the drama. There are three aspects of reality, namely the creator, the created, and the individual who comprehends the former two. Similarly, the dramatist and the actors make up for the creation aspect of the drama, about the spectators who offer a nuanced but psychological point of view.

A drama that connects the dramatist, actors, and spectators, would be ineffective in serving its purpose of providing entertainment without the most vital component of the process. It is called *Rasa*. In Sanskrit, *Rasa* is variedly used to mean quality, essence, and a particular taste. But in the aesthetic sense, *Rasa* means the aesthetic object required for an aesthetic experience (*Rasasvada*) [21]. It is through *Rasa* that the three constituents involved in a drama, namely, music, dance, and acting are justified. The three constituents are the presentation of *Rasa*, without which a drama won't be a drama in the most astute sense.

Before discussing the Advaita theory on *Rasavada*, a clear distinction needs to be made between essence and *Rasa*. Essence is the unifying component of the natural creative process that does not involve any artificial or human intervention and is the organic worth for all of creation. Rasa is found only in the aesthetic form that is purposefully worked upon for the spectator's delight, besides satisfying its creators while creating it. Unlike the essence, which represents unity or an organic whole, *Rasa* represents unity amidst multiplicity or diversity [22].

While using approximate qualifications to describe Brahman, as to what experiencing it could be, one of the most common denotations used is '*Ananda*'. The meaning of '*Ananda*' is bliss and the experience of Brahman, which according to the idealism and monism of Advaita Vedanta, occurs when one taps into the eternal harmony of the universe. This is to say that Brahman is *Ananda* because one experiences in Brahman the eternal rest and blissfulness that arises because of the realization of that condition that everything is in a continuous state of harmony.

Dissonance occurs because we not only fail to experience the harmony but in place of it, create orchestrated realities. According to Shankara, it is on account of our *Avidya-Kama-Karma*, or the desires arising out of the conflict because of the ignorance that binds us, and the harmony is replaced by conditioned realities that supersede common experience, forcing it to misunderstand the sensible reality to be the ultimate truth. This very word '*Ananda*' holds the key to understanding the aesthetic theory of Vedanta [23].

The only possible way to experience this *Ananda* is through *Jivamukti*, and to a *Jivanmukta*, although he is sensually receptive, yet his senses, fail to affect his significant achievement. According to Advaita, true beauty is not in worldly impressions, nor are they perfect for that matter. The only perfection in beauty is identical with ultimate reality and that is the real beauty. But in the light of its experience, this revelation is reserved only for that knower who has acquired *Jnana*. Real beatitude can neither be expressed vernacularly nor be understood objectively [24]. It can only be experienced through realization.

Any art in its full form and glory intends to serve a primary purpose, that being an experiential delight for those who witness it. To an artist, nothing gives more pleasure than his art being acknowledged and appreciated for what it truly is, an honest attempt. For that, the artist must work through a sense of detachment to the outcome of his art and to be fully indulged in the process. This sense of detachment serves a dual purpose. Firstly, a desire to master a particular art form by focusing on its aspects like symmetry for architecture, rhythm for music, and *Rasa* for drama that helps the artist progress from strength to strength until he has created a masterpiece. Secondly, while trying to master a craft, by focusing on the aspects that make up the form, the artist manages to keep all those aspects together by securing unity in the subject matter, i.e. his art form.

In the Advaita sense, the knower experiences the ultimate form of beauty in Brahman. Yet up until a certain point, he may still experience nature's diversity without being affected by it. For the knower, unity in the diverse nature accounts for what is beautiful to him. Likewise, for an artist, it is the whole idea of creating beautiful art. However, searching for beauty in art which is still a human creation, is still a lower level of search. A beautiful art form is only a justification for a search for perfection by the artist. The same attitude can be compared with a *Jivanmukta*, who gets a glimpse of *Moksha* but is not truly *Mukta* in the Advaita sense [25].

Pleasure or delight (*Preeti*) from art is not the only concern of the artist, nor is the only purpose of its creation. In the more philosophic sense, the true purpose of a particular art form is to provide an overall experience of aesthetics of which delight is the first one. The valuation of art is assigned over an active period and evaluated continuously [26]. Sentimental satisfaction is only a defining characteristic of that value. The idea of immersing oneself into the art signifies a particular frame of mind and attitude towards one's work which does not necessarily pin on pleasure as the ultimate goal.

Rather, it creates a matured sense of 'disinterestedness', on account of which he intends to express and not impress through his form. According to Prof. Hiriyanna, this also invokes a sense of compassion and insight for the artist and he maintains an idealistic yet unique stance.

For all its experience, art cannot be considered the ideal one, because it suffers a deficiency, that being the experience is temporary. The pleasure of art lasts until it can stimulate the senses. And no stimulus can last forever, because it is always relative to the extraneous conditions and based on a fabricated situation for its setting created by the artist. [27]. So, what is the point of art? The effect created by an art form may leave a lasting impression but does not last forever. So, is it not ultimately a deceit? An art form is structured in such a way that it finds unity amidst extraneous conditions of the diverse and varied reality that is in its scope. By doing so, it inculcates an optimistic attitude of disinterestedness and is hence impersonal. It may seem personal for the delight it brings as an immediate effect. But a true artist indulges in his art a sense of forgetfulness and spontaneous joy. This is an aesthetic fulfillment that art caters to, and that experience scales much higher above the everyday mundane experiences of the common life.

Critics of Hindu philosophy often use similar analogies while criticizing the actual conditions for the reality of this world as described by Advaita.

Whether the world was purposefully created or not, if the world is unreal, how can one produce evidence for a creator? If the world is an illusion, how can there be a definite way to salvation from this world? Advaita critic Richard W Brooks says, that "the doctrine that the world is an illusion is itself an illusion". If the world is an illusion, how can the Advaita way as proposed by Shankara be real since it is of this world and everything in it is an illusion? If everything is an illusion, can anything be truly beautiful? But Advaita maintains that the world has some reality to it because it is cognized. Yet what was the purpose behind its creation? Badarayana solves the problem of illusion by invoking *'Lila'*, a divine play or a cosmic drama where the world is neither purposefully created nor purposeless [28]. Creation as it so happens, is the work of *Ishvara*, who also annihilates it in due time. Meanwhile, his process of creation is not a motivated activity nor a disinterested eventual outcome. Rather, it is a free, spontaneous, and joyous creative process and a release of energy without any active participation.

Shankara has compared the *Lila* to the breathing activity that is essential to a sentient being's physical existence [29]. The process of breathing, as it so happens, is a natural process, taking the course of law of its nature, and is without any extraneous intervention. Yet there is shortened breathing in high altitudes, and fast breathing after strenuous physical activity when one consciously tries to influence his breathing process. But such scenarios are short-lived as long as the conditions prevail. The process returns to the original status quo, wherein breathing is a spontaneous process, that happens to indicate that someone is alive. Similarly, the activity of *Ishvara*, indicating the creative process, is a mere sport, a drama, that is performed, out of its own sake, and not to serve a purpose.

Unlike the other Hindu traditions, Shankara does not admit to the complete authority of this cosmic drama, since this play is only a provisional explanation for unveiling the cosmic ignorance or Maya of the apparent or illusive reality [30]. Sankara's use of the play theme is applicable only in the phenomenal reality and is part of lower knowledge that is only *Vyavaharika Satya*. According to Shankara, the nature of play is such that it can only bring forth joy and delight.

When played for the sake of playing, a play serves the dual purpose of satisfying the players and the spectators. Similarly, for a *Jivanmukta*, who is the one free or *Mukta* while still living, there is but only one ideation of Brahman, and that being 'Brahman is real and is everywhere and in everything'. In an aesthetical sense, this is the realization before the actual realization (*Moksha*), which is achieved through *Jnana* or ultimate knowledge. To be able to experience the same ecstasy and bliss for everything and in everything is to say that the conditions for what is beautiful consummate and find their amalgamation into a singular monistic confirmation that everything is beautiful the way it is.

6.3 Comparative Analysis

When Buddhism was born in India around the sixth century BCE, it happened as a reaction against certain Brahminic practices and prejudices that dominated the Indic society of that time. The word Buddha comes from the Sanskrit verb Budh, which translated from the Vedic scriptures means 'to know' or 'to wake up'. So, Buddha means a person who knows or one who woke up. The importance of becoming the Buddha means that there is an individual who knows the truth, not because it was revealed to him through the divine inscription of the scriptures, but because he knows so, by experiencing it outside the accepted customs, norms, and methods set by the Brahmanical society.

When Buddhism spread to China, the word Buddha was understood as 'the awakened one'. To the Chinese mind, the Buddha was someone, who with a profound insight and understanding of his self-nature had awakened from his slumber by following the 'Way', and not through the study and speculation of scriptures. In his 'Way', there was also hope for the common man to desire liberation. The Buddha said that the sinner and the saint both had an equal shot at Nirvana. So, all forms of segregation based on physical conditions are an antithesis to the equality and freedom for all of humanity.

Buddhism was born to oppose and invalidate the Vedic absolutism, and not to offer a Buddhist point of view [31]. In doing so, the Buddha rejected the notion of self (*Atman*) of Brahminism and posited the non-self (*Anatman*) doctrine. Unlike his critics, he did not impose his ideas which were diametrically opposite to others. Buddhism was not an independent discovery, but a situational reform that Buddha had aimed for. Closely associated is the concept of impermanence (*Anitya*). The Buddha said that all things are in a state of ceaseless change because their nature is transformed continuously and hence, they are unable to hold on to their identity. Things are impermanent because they change from moment to moment. Things are devoid of any fixed identity and because of this, there is no essential quality in things. This is true in the case of both physical objects and physiological phenomena.

The third cornerstone of Buddhism is the genesis of inter-being or dependent origination (*Pratitasamuchyapada*). It implies that, amidst the impermanent, non-essential world of suffering, there is a silver lining, which is the dependency and interpenetration of one thing into another. The presence of one thing (*Dharma*) is the confirmation of the presence of all things other [32]. With these three facets of truth, the Buddha did not establish them as an absolute authority but asked to do the most important thing of all, which is to directly experience it. This is where the

Buddhist notion of aesthetics, particularly through Zen can be highlighted.

According to Zen, to be able to intuitively appreciate the beauty in the transientness of *Dharma* in the physical world is the appropriate admiration for the irreversible flow of life and matter in the spiritual world. According to the twelfth-century Vietnamese Zen monk Dao Hanh, 'If one thing exists, so does everything, even a grain of dust' [33]. The explanation for this in the aesthetic sense means that the ability to perceive all things as they are and call them perfect is to truly understand the meaning of beauty amidst an impermanent, non-essential, and imperfect world. The philosophic and moral intentions of the religious fraternity of our times have a somewhat perverted interpretation of the truth. In such crucial times, an insightful analysis of the nature of beauty and love can correct the distorted images that we have regarding ourselves and others because mere intellectualization cannot fully satisfy the spiritual aspiration in most people. One needs a common standard of how to look at all things, in the presence of which, the 'what' to look for, becomes secondary. And then, even one will find hope in despair.

In the Indian context, however, aesthetics is separately studied along with the course of history and philosophy and is applied to experience the absolute in a limited capacity. The average spiritual journey does not just end with the attainment of knowledge but to be truly able to implement the acquired knowledge as a practical solution to the problems of life. But making it a 'way of life' is the real goal of the spiritual pursuit in the most pragmatic sense. The philosophical axioms of sensing knowledge, experiencing knowledge, and implementing knowledge have included two most important variable factors called ethics and aesthetics, both of which share an interdependent kinship. Both ethics and aesthetics aim to improve and influence human life, with the help of philosophical knowledge.

The Indian thought process studies the idea of goodness with the concept of beauty together in close relation. Based on the axioms, a foundational doctrine in the Indian philosophic system developed which posited that there is but one absolute reality, and it essentially is a manifestation of itself into the world. This manifestation is more vivid and recognizable within man in his innermost self (*Atman*), and not so much outside of him, which briefly is an illusion-based reality [34]. The idea that dominated the Indian thought process is that the quest for ultimate reality should be directed inwards, for the reality is the same as man's self. The goal of existence is to serve fully here in this life, before being completely taken off from serving ever again. One has to be a *Jivanmukta* before *Moksha* and that is the definition of true freedom. One finds harmony in freedom, not by suppressing instincts but by purifying them into passionless interests. A dispassionate activity, by definition, will be good, and the eventual outcome will be because of an unbiased pursuit of excellence, born out of love for the overall act.

Closely related to the ethical approach is the aesthetic experience, which in Advaita is expanded to understand the absolute. To indulge in art is to be able to dedicate one's life to the pursuit of its mastery. But to do so, one must be able to distinguish that the blissful state one experiences when being submerged in art is a glimpse of what it could be when the absolute is realized. But where does art originate from? The Advaita explanation is that art originates from the sphere of consciousness which is the transcendent reality *Sat-Cit-Ananda* [35]. Beyond the surface appearance of a particular artwork and the mere superficial understanding of an art form, there is an insightful understanding that is the idea of art arising from the artist's inner being. It is from the space of his consciousness which is aligned with the universal consciousness that he draws his initial inspiration from. The artist may not be even aware of this, but something motivates him to bring an idea into an image, to find a reference to a sense, or to make an art into a form. It can be argued that since the source of origin of art is consciousness itself, a particular art form, however culturally biased, has hidden intentionality to be aesthetically impactful, meaningful beyond what meets the eye, and truly beautiful below the surface [36]. This argument gives the impression that the art is somewhat alive, conscious, and intentional. But to see it for what it is, i.e. a projection of consciousness, one has to approach it through intuition.

There is a reason why, a particular form of art like a painting looks very ugly at first viewing, but gets sold for unimaginable prices. Similarly, a drama may be commercially panned but critically acclaimed. What is the reason behind these two distinctive points of view? What do some people see in an art that others don't? The answer is *Rasa*. In the Advaita sense, *Rasa* is the expression of universal emotion over personal ones drawn from the subtle understanding of life [37]. Any form of art will have both conformists appreciating it and critics panning it. But what connects the experiencers, the artist, and the art form itself, is the idea that there is unity amidst diversity. This unity is brought forth by *Rasa* which fully represents it.

Advaita also speaks of a higher form of *Rasa* known as

Shantarasa which is the true essence of all aesthetic pleasure [38]. According to Elliot Deutsch, there is a dynamic harmony in all beings and of all becoming. And that is silence. So, *Shantarasa* in a much more insightful understanding, is the silence that comes after a deep understanding of the art form, for what it is behind the surface traits [39]. The experience of this *Shantarasa* is the highest form of appreciation that can be used in art, which surprisingly is not expressed at all. It is a silent confirmation that the experiencer has truly grasped the beauty of the form, more so than anyone else, and it happens in silence. Similarly, to be able to have a glimpse of the self or the absolute, through an expression of bliss (*Ananda*) or aesthetic pleasure, is the right comparison of what it means to truly appreciate an art, and what it means to faintly experience the absolute.

The aesthetic principle of *Shantarasa* can be compared with *Satori* in Zen Buddhism, which is a profound and transcendent experience beyond any words. Just like *Shantarasa* reflects the emotional essence experienced in the aesthetic encounter, *Satori* signifies sudden enlightenment or the moment of awakening beyond any intellectual understanding. Both Zen Buddhism and Advaita Vedanta share a common quest of the search for beauty below the surface. Both traditions seek a deeper understanding and appreciation for true reality beyond superficial appearances. True recognition of beauty happens beyond what meets the eye. Yet true beauty is always in front of the eye. The recognition is to see that which has always been in front of you.

References

1. *Zen Buddhism and Its Relation to Art*, Arthur Waley, page21
2. Ibid, page-24

3. *Ethics and Aesthetics are One: The Case of Zen Aesthetics,* H. Bai, 1997

4. *Art Experience,* Mysore Hiriyanna, Page-24

5. *On Understanding Rasa in the Tradition of Advaita Vedanta,* Dr. K.S.Sivakumar, 2017

6. *Ibid*

7. *Zen aesthetic: development and influence in culture and contemporary painting of China, Japan, and USA,* Zeng Xi

8. *The Aesthetic Pleasure of Everyday Life: An Exploration through the Buddhist Concept of Vikalpa,* Priyadarshi Patnaik

9. *Towards the Beauty of Buddhism: The Development and Validation of as Buddhist Aesthetics Scale,* Yao Song & Zhenzhen Qin

10. *The Unknown Craftsman: A Japanese Insight into Beauty,* Soetsu Yanagi, Page-129

11. *Ibid,* Page-130

12. *Ibid,* Page-147

13. *Wabi-Sabi,* Richard Martin, page-15

14. *Ibid,* Page-16

15. *Ibid,* Page-152

16. *Ibid,* Page-154

17. *The Beauty of Everyday Things,* Soetsu Yanagi, Page-52

18. *Ibid,* Page-53

19. *Comparative Aesthetics, Vol-1. Indian Aesthetics,* Dr. Kanti Chandra Pandey, Page-1

20. *A Bird's-Eye View of Indian Aesthetics*, K. Pandey
21. *Comparative Aesthetics, Vol-1. Indian Aesthetics*, Dr. Kanti Chandra Pandey, Page-20
22. Ibid, Page-22
23. *Art Experience*, Mysore Hiriyanna, Page-8
24. Ibid, Page-9
25. Ibid, Page-10
26. Ibid, Page-24
27. *The Quest after Perfection*, M. Hiriyanna, page 50
28. *Playful Illusion: The Making of Worlds in Advaita Vedanta*, Frederic F Fost, 1998
29. Ibid
30. Ibid
31. *Zen Keys*, Thich Nhat Hanh, Page-37
32. Ibid, Page-41
33. Ibid, Page-41
34. *Art Experience*, Mysore Hiriyanna, Page-3
35. *Connecting Art with Spirituality within the Indian Aesthetics of Advaita Vedanta*, Ross Keating
36. Ibid 37. Ibid 38. Ibid 39. Ibid

Chapter 7

Practice

7.0 Introduction

In the previous chapters, we compared and contrasted the unique philosophy of Zen Buddhism and Advaita Vedanta, each showing a different face of a similar truth. In this chapter, we are going to focus on the practice aspects of Zen Buddhism and Advaita Vedanta. In Zen, the focus is on mindfulness practice by emphasizing disciplined meditation and the cultivation of awareness in everyday activities. The goal is to develop and observe a deep sense of presence in the present that leads to a sense of awareness in each moment. With prolonged practice, it leads a practitioner to insight, enlightenment, and a direct experience of the reality that is beyond any intellectual grasp.

In Advaita Vedanta, the focus is on the practice that leads to the understanding of 'oneness' or nonduality. All practices are centered around the idea that everything is fundamentally interconnected and indivisible, and that there is no real separation between the individual self or *Atman* and the universal consciousness or Brahman. The practices primarily involve deep meditation and contemplation, rigorous self-inquiry, and studying of the sacred texts. The goal is to realize this divine unity, transcend the illusion of any individual identity, and recognize the underlying interconnectedness and thus the oneness of all existence.

The task of comparing the practice aspects of both traditions entails looking at the institutional framework of the sects, their main scriptures used during practice, and the liturgical aspects of the practice. Special vehicles such as Koans are employed in Zen practice. Advaita Vedanta, however, prioritizes the importance of scriptural study, and relentless contemplation based on such study. The primary tools employed in Advaita Vedanta are philosophical teachings, guided meditations, and discussions that center around the nature of reality, the status of self, and the validity of ultimate truth.

7.1 Zen practice

Zen Buddhism is practiced in China since the sixth century CE. The practice spread to the neighboring countries of Korea, Vietnam, and Japan a couple of hundred years thereafter, Japan being the last one where Zen practice started in the twelfth century CE by the Japanese master Eisai. Zen spread to Europe and the Americas after the Second World War, primarily due to the efforts of the Japanese. In the interconnected world of the twenty-first century, Zen practice is spreading all over the world.

Integral to Zen practice are the Zen institutions that serve as the anchor in guiding the Zen practice. The scriptures and liturgy generally used become other important aspects of Zen. Starting from about the tenth century CE, and up to the present time, the Koans have been a part of Zen, varying in the extent of their application depending upon the particular sects. Meditation practice is the most important part of Zen practice. All of these areas will be dealt with in this section.

7.1.1 Zen Institutions

Zen Buddhism has been practiced in the East Asian countries of Japan, Korea, Vietnam, and China for about a thousand years and more. The European countries and the Americas have been exposed to Zen since the twentieth century. There are differences in the Zen institutions between each of the countries in terms of sutras, mantras, and images used during services and the type of Zen institutions.

We will first consider in more detail the Zen institutions prevalent at present in Japan and the United States to give a better understanding of what is prevalent now.

Zen Temples

The Soto Zen sect has about fifteen thousand temples spread throughout Japan and is more prevalent in the rural areas for serving the farming communities. The Rinzai Zen sect was first brought to Japan in the twelfth century CE to serve the Samurai and the ruling communities of Japan in Kyoto and Kamakura and has about six thousand temples spread all over the urban areas [1]. These Zen temples provide different services to the members of the community in a particular geographical area. All of the death-related memorial services are performed at the Zen temples. In the garden attached to the temples, there is usually a separate bundle of bamboo sticks for each family, and there is a separate bamboo stick for each departed member of the family in that bundle. Services are held in the temple in the memory of departed family members.

The Buddha Hall is the chamber where the image of the Sakyamuni Buddha is kept along with some of the Bodhisattvas, such as Samanta Bhadra, Kshittigarbha, and Ananda. An adjoining meditation hall is where the members of the temple do Zazen or sitting meditation. This is a multipurpose hall which is also used as the dining hall and the resting area. There are separate kitchen and bathroom facilities too.

Zen Monasteries

The Rinzai sect administers its six thousand temples through affiliations with fifteen head temples or monasteries:

1. Myoshinji in Kyoto
2. Nan zen-ji in Kyoto
3. Tenryu-ji in Kyoto
4. Tofoku-ji in Kyoto
5. Kenin-ji in Kyoto
6. Daitoku-ji in Kyoto
7. Shokoku-ji in Kyoto
8. Hoko-ji in Hamamatsu
9. Eigen-ji in Higoshiohmi
10. Kogaku-ji in Yamanashi
11. Butsu-ji in Mihara, Hiroshima
12. Kencho-ji in Kamakura
13. Engaku-ji in Kamakura
14. Kokutai-ji in Tataoka, Hokuriku
15. Manpuku-ji in Kyoto

Myoshin-ji is the largest Rinzai monastery with three thousand plus temples affiliated with it. Manpuku-ji is the head temple of the Obaku sect which is usually included in the Rinzai school.

The Soto Zen sect has two head temples that control all the temples and monasteries.

1. Soji-ji at Tsurumi Yokohama has almost fourteen thousand temples and monasteries affiliated. It was established in 1321 CE. There are about thirty teaching monasteries where monks are trained.
2. Ethei-ji in Fukui Prefecture is the head temple

established by Dogen Zenji, the founder of the Soto sect in Japan. It was established in 1244 CE and has a handful of temples affiliated to it. The original temple Kosho-ji which was started by Dogen at Uji near Kyoto is still functioning today.

The Soto sect divides the temples into five categories:

1. Head Temple (Honzan)
2. Teaching Monastery (Kikuchi)
3. Dharma Temple (Ho chi)
4. Ordinary Temples (Jun Ho chi)

The Soto sect has developed the following three documents for the management of the temples:

1. Sotoshu Constitution (Sotoshushuken)
2. Regulations for the Religion Judicial Person (Sotoshu)
3. Sotoshu Standard Procedures (Sotoshukitel)

Most of the Zen institutions in the United States are temple cum monasteries that serve members of the local community and other participating members from anywhere in North America. The following Rinzai Zen temple cum monasteries are functioning now in the United States:

1. Rinzai-ji in California
2. Dai Botsu Zendo Kongo-ji in New York
3. Chozen-ji in Hawaii
4. Daiyuzen-ji in Illinois
5. Konin-ji in Wisconsin

6. Chobo-ji in Washington
7. Cold Mountain Zen in New Jersy

The following Soto temple cum monasteries are functioning in the United States:

1. Shasta Abbey, Shasta Mountain, California
2. Tassajara Zen Mountain Centre, California
3. Zen Center of San Fransisco
4. Zen Center of Chicago, Illinois
5. Zen Center of Los Angeles, California

There are monasteries that neither follow the practice of Rinzai nor Soto sects, but have adopted practices that are suitable for the American environment:

1. Rochester Zen Center, Rochester, New York
2. Zen Mountain Monastery, Mt. Temper, New York

Zen Sangha

Sangha or communities of Zen practitioners are developed around the Zen temples and the monasteries. However, there are no Zen temples and monasteries in smaller cities and towns to provide support for meetings and meditation. Hence, a sangha is formed of Zen practitioners to meet at a certain facility at least once a week. The sangha attracts people of diverse backgrounds around a geographical area. The sangha often plans elaborate retreats for one or more days. They may also plan separate socio-religious functions for the members of the group. Generally, a house-holder man or woman, with experience and training in Zen meditation, leads such a group.

The internet has become the universal information network all over the world, and people are exposed to Zen ideology and practice through the internet and the media. Hence, Zen sangha is organized first in geographical areas where there aren't any Zen temples.

7.1.2 Zen Scriptures

There are Mahayana sutras that are often read, discussed, and chanted during Zen practice:

1. Heart Sutra or Prajna Paramita Hridaya Sutra
2. Diamond Sutra or Vajrachhedika Sutra
3. Lotus Sutra or Saddharma Pundarika Sutra
4. Lankavatara Sutra
5. Avatamsaka Sutra or Flower Garland Sutra
6. Vimalakirti Sutra
7. Platform Sutra of the Sixth patriarch

These sutras are briefly summarized in this section.

Heart Sutra

Prajna Paramita Hridaya Sutra or the Heart Sutra is the most famous of all the Mahayana Sutras. It is a fourteen *Sloka* or verse version summary of the Prajna-Paramita Shastra that has versions ranging up to a hundred thousand verses. In Heart Sutra, Avalokitesvara addresses Buddha's chief disciple Shari Putra to express his own experience of attaining *Prajna* or wisdom [3.4,5,6].

- That the five *Skandhas* defining the sentient beings are all empty, i.e., bereft of any self- nature (Swabhava)
- All beings and phenomena are created only in the presence of other phenomena. This is called

conditioned origination or *Pratitya Samutpada*. People can escape rebirth and suffering by eliminating desires thus attaining *Nirvana*.

- The six senses (eyes, ears, nose, tongue, body, and mind), the corresponding six types of sense objects (form, sound, smell, taste, touch, and thought), and the consequent six types of consciousness are all empty.
- Following the six *Paramitas*, one attains wisdom, but wisdom and the fruits of wisdom are similarly empty. Since there are no fruits to be gained, the Bodhisattva is free from deluding obstacles and is dependent on *Prajna-Paramita*. Since there is no mental pain or suffering, the Bodhisattva reaches *Nirvana*.

Diamond Sutra

Vajrachhedika Sutra is known as Diamond Sutra and is very much revered in the Zen and Vajrayana sects. The Sixth Patriarch Hui Neng is supposed to have reached *Satori* after listening to this sutra. It is a conversation between the Buddha and his senior disciple Subhuti [7,8,9].

- Diamond Sutra cuts through all kinds of concepts just like a diamond.
- Bodhisattva does not think of any attachment at the time of showing compassion.
- All forms in this material world are false.
- We should never be attached to any words or things. The words spoken by the Buddha are like a boat. Once the river is crossed, we have to leave behind the boat. Ultimate truth cannot be understood through the medium of words or by thinking.

- Only a demonstration of the truth can be called the truth.
- Everything is like the flickering morning star.
- Everything is like the lightening in the blue sky
- Everything is like a bubble in the water.
- Everything is like a dream in the night.

Lotus Sutra

Saddharma Pundarika Sutra is known as the Lotus Sutra. Kumarajiva had translated the original Sanskrit version to Chinese in 406 CE and it had twenty-eight chapters. Lotus Sutra is the most important and popular sutra in East Asia since many of the Buddhist sects were started there with Lotus Sutra as their foundation. Chih-I, the founder of the Tien-tai sect in China, proclaimed in the sixth century CE that the Lotus Sutra is the highest and the last teaching of the Buddha delivered from the Gridhrakutta mountain near Rajagriha. Hence Tien-tai sect also was known as the Lotus school. This sect spread to Japan in the eighth century and was known there as the Tendai sect. Tendai sect remained the primary Buddhist sect of Japan for almost five hundred years and provided the foundation for many Buddhist leaders who started new Buddhist sects based on the Lotus Sutra or otherwise. Thus Dogen, Nichiren, Honen, Shin Ran, etc. were all started in the Tendai sect. Lotus sutra communicates the following messages [10,11,12]:

- Buddha shows three paths towards

Nirvana. In *Shravakayana*, one listens to all the teachings given by the Buddha and thus achieves *Nirvana*.

In Pratyekabuddhayana, one achieves *Nirvana* through one's learnings and discipline. In Bodhisattvayana, one adopts the path of the Boddhisattva to uplift the whole world to achieve *Nirvana*.

- Lotus sutra also says that all beings have Buddha nature and can achieve enlightenment. An ordinary person can achieve enlightenment by the sheer power of faith and devotion. Even a person who has not taken the vow to become a monk can attain enlightenment by demonstrating faith and devotion.
- Lotus sutra introduces the concept of Trikaya philosophy, whereby the Buddha is portrayed as *Nirmanakaya* or the historical Buddha, as the *Sambhogakaya* or the one with additional physical and spiritual qualities for teaching the disciples, and finally as the *Dharmakaya*, the sum total of all the sentient beings and things of the universe.
- Lotus sutra also introduces few parables that illustrate moral principles. Some of the important parables are:
  - A burning house where the owner is bringing out his playing children by promising them things according to their specific likings.
  - A prodigal son, poor and hating himself, slowly comes to know that he has plenty of wealth.
  - An unreal city, where the leader takes the people following him through a difficult route by tempting the existence of a beautiful unreal city as the destination.

Lankavatara Sutra

A copy of the Lankavatara Sutra was given by

Bodhidharma to his disciple Heiko and for several hundred years it was used to train the Zen monks in China. The Southern Chinese branch of Zen headed by Hui Neng used the Diamond sutra as the primary scripture and did not make special use of the Lankavatara sutra. This sutra is also a long and complex sutra of more than three hundred pages. It has imbibed in it all of the main ideas of Buddhism and Zen. Since the topics are not introduced in any systematic manner, it is difficult to follow the text without the guidance of a very experienced master. When thousands of disciples started joining Zen at the time of Hui Neng, it was not possible to use the Lankavatara sutra as the teaching vehicle and its usage declined rapidly in Zen. However, it has always been a very important sutra for experienced Zen followers and is used today to advance in the path of enlightenment. The following main teachings are included in the Lankavatara sutra [13,14,15]:

- Everything we experience in this world is a projection of our mind only. Zen points directly at our mind and pushes us towards experiencing reality. *Vijnana* or consciousness is the fifth *Skandha* that defines a sentient being and there are six types of consciousness corresponding to the six sense organs (eye, ear, nose, tongue, body, and mind). A seventh consciousness called *Manas* is added to denote our false consciousness of self. An eighth consciousness called *Alaya Vijnana* is also added to denote all the seeds planted corresponding to our past actions. This is known as Chitta-Matra, or Mind-Only philosophy, or Vijnanavada.

- All sentient beings have Buddha nature imbibed in them and they are capable of germinating this seed planted in them.

- The Buddha is represented in three bodies for the welfare of the people of the world.
  - *Nirmanakaya* is the Shakyamuni Buddha who came to this world as a human being to teach the *Dharma*.
  - *Sambhogakaya* is the body of delight that represents the Buddha with all the thirty-two major marks and eighty minor marks shown for teaching the Bodhisattvas.
  - *Dharmakaya* is the essence of the universe and it has represented the teachings expounded by the Buddha.
- Sentient beings and things do not have any inherent self-nature or Swabhava. The cause of all suffering is due to the false notion of having a self-nature.
- All things are unborn or *Anatpada* because they are manifestations of the mind only.
- Bodhisattva Dasha Bhumi describes how one can go through the ten stages of development of a Bodhisattva.
- The dictum 'beyond words and letters', says that words and letters cannot exhaust the meaning inherent in reality. Intellectual analysis of the sutra alone cannot lead one to enlightenment.

Avatamsaka Sutra

Avatamsaka or Garland sutra is one of the most popular sutras in Mahayana Buddhism and was the foundation for the Hua Yen school of Buddhism in China. It was also influential in Chan or Zen Buddhism. The following is a summary of the main texts in the sutra [16,17].

- Dasha Bhumika part of the sutra talks about the ten stages of development for a Bodhisattva. This is the same as described in the Lankavatara sutra. In addition, it talks about the development of *Bodhichitta* that leads to the attainment of Buddhahood.

- Ganda Vyuha part of the sutra shows that all phenomena in the universe are empty and infinitely interpenetrating leading to a perception of fields of assemblies and beings. That the world is like a dream in the mind, and the Buddhas are mere reflections, and the phenomena are like an echo. The Buddhas, through their infinite power and omnipotence, create an infinite number of forms. The Buddhas through their teachings lead sentient beings through the Bodhisattva stages and finally to Buddhahood. As the climax, it describes the pilgrimage of the layman Sudhana to various lands to find a suitable teacher to instruct him on the ways of the Bodhisattva.

Vimala Kirti Sutra

It is about a lay Buddhist person who attained a high degree of enlightenment. This sutra had a definite influence on Zen. The sutra teaches through the story of Vimala Kirti, a merchant householder of Vaishali who plays sick to attract visitors, to whom he teaches enlightenment. Shari Putra and Manjusri are sent to inquire about his illness. The following is a summary of its teaching [18,19]:

- The world as seen is a mere illusion. Everything we see is devoid of self-essence or self-nature and hence empty. All *Dharmas* have a single ultimate quality and are non-dual.

- The path of Mahayana, is superior to all other paths,

Shravakayana and *Hinayana*.

- The sutra is perhaps best known for the silence of Vimala Kirti. In an assembly of Bodhisattvas, everyone was asked to explain non-duality. The last Bodhisattva to answer was Manjusri and he said that all of them had fallen into dualism by answering. Vimala Kirti on his turn, remained silent. Silence was his answer.

This sutra had a profound influence on Zen through Vimala Kirti's silence, that words cannot communicate the ultimate reality.

Platform Sutra of the Sixth Patriarch

Patriarch Hui Neng talks about the stories about him and the teachings ascribed to him. It is a collection of early Chan teachings from the eighth century CE. Following is a summary of the sutra [20].

- Fifth patriarch Hung Jen invites his disciples wanting to succeed him to write a poem demonstrating that they had achieved enlightenment. Shen Shui, the leading disciple writes on the corridor wall the poem:

  ➤ The body is the Bodhi tree, The mind is like a bright mirror's stand,

  At all times we must strive to polish it,

  And must not let dust collect.

Hui Neng, who was illiterate, heard the poem read to him and composed the following stanza to write on the corridor.

➤ *Bodhi* originally is not a tree,

The mirror has no stand,

Buddha - nature is always clear and pure,

Where is the room for dust?

The mind is the *Bodhi* tree,

The body is the bright mirror's stand,

The bright mirror is original,

Where could there be any dust?

Hui Neng's poem alludes to the intuitive sudden nature of the realization, as opposed to the constant practice proposed by Shen Shui for a gradual attainment of enlightenment. Hui Neng's so-called 'sudden enlightenment school' in Southern China eventually eclipsed Shen Shui's Northern school of 'gradual enlightenment'. The sutra also consists of the following:

- *Prajna* or wisdom is attained when the mind comes to a state of 'thoughtlessness' as a result of proper meditation.
- Hui Neng relates the story of Bodhidharma telling Emperor Wu of Liang that his building of many Buddhist temples brought no merit. What is important is whether one's inner state of purity is exposed.
- That meditation is the essence of wisdom and that wisdom is the foundation of meditation.
- Our fundamental state is pure and it is not attained by concentrating the mind on purity during meditation, but rather by just doing seated meditation.
- It relates different stories of encounters and dialogues described by Hui Neng.

7.1.3 Zen Liturgy

During Zen services in the sangha, temples, and monasteries prayers and songs are chanted in addition to the sutras. Different vows are also taken during the religious ceremonies. Reverence is shown towards different Buddhas and Bodhisattvas. In this section, we will discuss in detail some of these things related to liturgical practice in Zen.

Prayers and Dharanis

The following prayer is offered after the food is served, just before eating, by taking morsels of food from everyone and then offering that along with the chants.

Prayers for offering food

- Namah-sarva-tathagata-avalokite!Om!

    Sambala Sambala!Om!

    Namah-Surupaya-Tathagataya!

    Tadyatha

    Om, Surupaya, Surupaya, Surupaya,

    Surupaya, Svaha!

    Namah-Samantabuddanam, Om!

    Namah-Ratnaketu-Tathagataya!

    Namah-Prabhutaratna-Tathagataya!

    Namah-Surupakaya-Tathagataya!

    Namah-Vipulakaya-Tathagataya!

    Namah-Avayankara-Tathagataya!

    Namah-Amitabha-tathagataya!

    Namah-Mitabhaya-Tathagataya!

Tadyatha, Amritabhave, Amritasidhe, Amritavikrante, Amrita-vikranta-gamine, Gaganakirtikare! Svaha!

Dharani for Removing Disasters (Sho-saimyo)

This is a hymn to goddess Kichijo or goddess Lakshmi of the Indic culture [21].

- Namo-Samanta-nataram

  Aprati-hatasya

  Saranam-tadyatha,

  Om, Khya-Khya-Khyahi-Khyahi Hum-hum-jvala-jvala-prajvala-prajvala Tista-tista stri-stri sphata-sphata, Kshantika-shriye Svaha!

Zen Songs

The Song of Zazen by Japanese Zen master Hakuin is chanted in the sangha and temples to praise Zazen practice. It is worth mentioning the last two stanzas [22]:

Our form becomes no form,

Without leaving we go and return,

Our thought becomes no thought,

Our song and dance become the voice of Dharma.

As the eternal tranquility of truth reveals,

We see the *Nirvana* in front of us,

This very place is the land of the lotus,

And this very body is the body of the Buddha.

Another poem of importance is Yoka Daishi's 'Song of Enlightenment'. He was one of the chief disciples of Hui

Neng, the sixth patriarch of Zen Buddhism. Here we quote the last two of the stanzas from 'Song of Enlightenment' [23]:

However rapidly revolves the iron-wheel over my head,

The perfect brightness of *Dhyana* and *Prajna* in me is never effaced;

The sun may turn cold and the moon hot,

With all the power of the evil ones, the true doctrine remains forever indestructible,

The elephant carriage steadily climbs up the steepest hill,

Before whose wheels how can the beetle stand?

The great elephant does not walk on the hare's lane,

Supreme enlightenment goes beyond the narrow range of intellection;

Cease from measuring heaven with a tiny piece of reed;

If you have no insight yet, I will have the matter settled for you.

Zen Vows and Precepts

Members of Zen fraternities take vows and chant acceptance of the precepts at different times during Zen services.

The **Refuge Vow** is taken at the beginning of events and ceremonies:

- *Buddham Sharanam Gachhami, Dharmam Sharanam Gachhami, Sangham Sharanam Gachhami*

  The Refuge Vow is repeated thrice.

The **Ten Grave Precepts** apply to all the followers of Zen, the lay persons, monks, and priests [24]:

1. Will not take any life and care for all
2. Will not steal and properly use other's properties
3. Will not misuse sex
4. Will not speak a lie
5. Will not misuse alcohol and drugs
6. Will not speak about the fault of others
7. Will not praise self or blame others. Overcome any weakness
8. Give spiritual and material help to others
9. Will not be angry and keep patience
10. Will not say anything bad about the three jewels of Buddhism and honor them

Zen functions are formally concluded by taking the four **Bodhisattva Vows**:

1. Save all sentient beings, although they are innumerable.
2. Control all the senses, although they are uncontrollable.
3. Learn the ways of the Dharma, although they are limitless.
4. Follow the path of the Buddha, although it is difficult.

Bodhisattva Vows are repeated thrice.

Zen Statues and Images

Different Bodhisattvas and Buddhas are depicted in

Zen institutions. Here we list a few of the important ones [25,26]:

Avalokitesvara is the most famous Bodhisattva in

Mahayana Buddhism and Zen. He is the embodiment of empathy for the suffering sentient beings. Avalokitesvara is also known as 'Kuan-yin' in China and 'Kwannon' in Japan.

Manjushri is the Bodhisattva of wisdom or *Prajna*. Manjushri is depicted with lotus flowers along with a copy of Prajna-Paramita Shastra near his head. He holds the sword of wisdom in one hand for the cutting off the ignorance.

Samantabhadra is the Bodhisattva who shows his spiritual influence throughout the world and saves the teachers of the *Dharma*. He travels on top of a white elephant with six teeth, representing the six sense organs in us. He keeps his six senses under control with the help of his wisdom. His emblem is the strolled paper where meditation sutras are written. Hence, he is also called the Bodhisattva of *Dhyana* and Zazen.

Kshittigarbha is the Bodhisattva who saves the people from suffering in hell and helps the dead children. He is also the savior of the pilgrims. Kshittigarbha is generally seen in the attire of a monk and holds a special monk's staff in one of his hands.

Maitreya is the Bodhisattva who would come as a Buddha in the future. He is supposed to be in Tushita heaven right now, waiting to come to this world. He is also the Bodhisattva of love and empathy. He is shown sitting on a high chair with his feet on the ground, signifying that he is ready to come to this world. He has the qualities of a man of action.

Akshobhya Buddha is the one who transforms our anger into a mirror-like wisdom. His color is blue, his symbol is the thunderbolt, and his transport is elephant. He is the lord of the eastern direction.

Ratnasambhava Buddha is the one who transforms our pride into wisdom of equilibrium. His color is faded gold, his symbol is the precious stone jewel and his transport is the horse. He is the lord of the southern direction.

Amitabha Buddha is the one who transforms our attachments and desires into a feeling of being one with them. His color is red, his symbol is the lotus flower, his transport is peacock and he is the lord of the western direction. By meditating on Amitabha Buddha, we are purified from the bondage and attain *Nirvana*.

Amoghasidhi Buddha is the lord of action who transforms any jealousy into a successful activity. His color is green, his symbol is double *Vajra* and his transport is Garuda, and he is the lord of the northern direction.

Vairochana Buddha throws light into our hearts to remove the darkness of ignorance. His color is white, his symbol is the golden wheel, his transport is the lion, and he is the lord of everywhere. He is regarded as the personification of *Dharmakaya*.

7.1.4 Zen Koans

Koan is an episode from the life of an ancient master pointing towards the realization of ultimate reality. Essential to each koan is a paradox that cannot be solved by reason and one must leap to a higher level of intuition to comprehend it. Hence, Koan is used to train the Zen student in this type of non-discursive thinking. The use of the Koans started in China in the tenth century and was formally publicized with the publication of Mu-Mon Kan in 1228 CE. It had a collection of forty-nine Koans collected by Zen master Mu-Mon [27].

There were other Koan collections around the same timeframe. Blue Cliff Record is a collection of hundred Koans by Chinese Masters [28,29]. YuanWu, or the Book of Serenity is the collection of enlightenment stories of one hundred Zen masters [30]. Shobogenzo is a collection of seventy-five Koans by Dogen Zenji of Japan [31].

There are about five to six hundred Koans that are generally used in the Zen community. Hakuin, the famous Rinzai Zen master of Japan, had classified the Koans into the following categories:

1. **Hoshin Koans** emphasize the unity of the universe by bringing the experience of 'emptiness'. Some of these Koans are:

   ➤ Joshu's Mu, asks one whether the dog has Buddha-nature.

   ➤ Hakuin's sound of clapping with only one hand.

   ➤ What was your face before your parents were born?

   ➤ Who is the one listening to the Koans?

2. **Kikan' Koans** emphasize the special characteristics of events and things. However, we have to look at these specialties from the perspective of 'oneness'. Everything is one and special at the same time. Examples of Kikan Koans are:

   ➤ Nansen cutting the cat

   ➤ All things return to one; to what does one return?

3. **Gonsen Koans** are the ones where we learn to use

words to express the feelings of transformation at the time of enlightenment. Examples of Gonsen Koans are:

- Joshu's 'wash the bowl'
- Yunmen's 'Every day is a good day'

4. **Hachi Nanto Koans** are difficult. Examples are:

- Buffalo passes through the enclosure
- The old woman burnt down the hut

5. **Goi Koans** are the ones where things are examined from the perspective of Tozan's Five Ranks. These are usually the last gates to go through to gain enlightenment.

6. **Kai Koans** show enlightened life from the perspective of sixteen behavioral edicts: The Three Refuge Precepts, the Three Pure Precepts, and the Ten Grave Precepts. These Koans are practiced before, during and after the '*Jukai*' process of administering the monkish vows.

7.1.5 Zen Meditation

Meditation is the foundation of Zen. Sitting meditation or Zazen practice is the most important activity that Zen practitioners have to go through. Both Rinzai and Soto Zen emphasize the Zazen practice. The Soto sect calls the Zazen practice '*Shikantaza*'. It says that *Shikantaza* should be a goal by itself and one should enjoy it as such, without the purposeful aim to reach enlightenment [32].

Meditation Posture

Proper physical posture during Zazen must be maintained to have good results. The upper body must be relaxed but the spine must be straight. The lower body must make firm and stable contact with the ground in a tripod. The buttocks resting at the end of the round meditation cushion or *Zafu*, and the two legs firmly touching the ground crossed in full or half lotus position (*Padmasana* or *Ardha Padmasana*). The feet should be pulled up as much as possible towards the trunk of the body. The soles of the feet must face upward. By sitting on the front edge of the *Zafu*, instead of at the center, the body is slightly slanted forward and the lower back is curved in. Rock forward and backward and sidewise until the body is in a centered position with the spine straight. In such a position, the tip of the nose would be in a straight vertical line with your navel. When the body is maintained in such an optimal position, the energy circulates naturally up the spine. The center of gravity of the body is at a point about two inches below the navel and it is called '*Tanden*' or '*Hara*'. If the body posture is centered around the *Hara*, then the upper body would feel light and be filled with energy.

If the lotus positions are not convenient, one can sit in the Burmese position where both the front legs are tucked in side by side on the ground. One can also sit in the *Vajrasana* position where you sit on top of the two feet curved backward with or without leaning backward and contacting the back of the chair. Any other position on the ground on the top of a hard pillow or *Zafu* would suffice also. The half lotus position is the most optimum position for Zazen in *Sesshins* where four to eight hours are spent daily in meditations. One can also alternately keep the left foot on the top instead of the right foot in the half lotus position and thus give more rest to the right foot.

The eyes should be kept half open and half gazing at the point about three feet ahead. Fully closing the eyes may lead to drowsiness. The two hands should rest on top of the legs, the left palm on top of the right palm, both positioning upwards, and the two thumbs touching each other making a circle underneath.

Breathing in Zazen

Proper Zazen posture of the body is essential to facilitate a deep level of breathing. Begin the Zazen process by first breathing out through the mouth and then breathing in through the nostrils. Continue this for several breaths, thus exhaling any extra air inside the stomach. Then move to inhaling and exhaling through the nostrils only. The breathing in and breathing out process feels as if it is happening from the *Tanden* or *Hara* in the lower abdomen. This is the first requirement during Zazen to do abdominal breathing. One should wear loose clothing so that the natural breathing process is not impeded.

Hara breathing or *Tanden Saku* is the most important part of Zazen and should be learned with practice.

Minding the Meditation

Meditation is started by breathing through the nostrils and the focus of the mind is kept completely on breathing without any break. When you inhale, just relax. But when you exhale, count each exhalation process mentally from one to ten. The focus of the mind is kept on the *Tanden*, observing how the abdomen is smoothly being filled up during the inhaling process and then slowly emptying during the exhalation. After a count of ten, the process is repeated five to ten times until the mind is completely still and there are no thoughts. After that counting is not necessary, but the attention is still on the inhaling and exhaling process as observed at the *Tanden*.

During the meditation process, if stray thoughts come to the mind, just recognize them and stop the thought. If there are any physical distractions like scratching etc., just recognize them and not indulge in them and go back to observing and counting the exhalation process [33,34, 35].

Koan Practice during Meditation

Koan practice is an essential part of the Rinzai Zen sect. It is less so in the Soto sect, although Koans are still used as an important device in Soto practice.

When a practitioner is working on the realization of a Koan, he can focus on the Koan during the meditation process, once the mind is settled to a quiet state and thus is no more counting of the breath. He is still aware of *Tanden* breathing, but simultaneously thinking on the Koan. The thinking about the Koan continues as he is out of the meditation and doing other things.

The Mu Koan is often used in the initial stages of Koan practice. As you breathe in and out during the meditation process, Mu is chanted silently synchronized with the breathing out process. As one goes deeper into the meditation, the Mu chant fades away and the cycles become longer and longer.

7.2 Advaita Vedanta Practice

Advaita Vedanta as a coherent religious sect started at the time of Adi Shankaracharya, but many of the practices were already prevalent from the time of the Upanishads.

Advaita Vedanta is a non-dualistic practice and is different from the dualistic Vedanta practice started by the followers of Ramanuja, Vallabha, etc.

The Kashmiri Shaivism practice is a non-dual practice but is different from Advaita Vedanta in many of the details.

In this section, we focus on the following five aspects of Advaita Vedanta practice:
1. Institutions developed for practice
2. Scriptures available
3. Liturgy employed
4. Stories and enquiries used
5. Meditation practice

7.2.1 Advaita Institutions

Advaita Vedanta has been practiced in India for more than a thousand years and is one of the main sects of Sanatana Dharma based upon the Vedas as the foundation. In the twentieth century, various Vedanta organizations established their centers in Europe and the Americas to spread the practice. Advaita Vedanta has also spread all over the world along with the Indian migrants.

Advaita Vedanta Temples

Followers of Advaita Vedanta need not attend any temples or worship any form of *Ishvara* and carry out all their strivings for right knowledge and *Moksha* at their homes. However, any temple of Shiva, Vishnu, Krishna, Rama, or Shakti Goddess can be used to express devotion, depending upon the preference of the practitioners. Adi Shankaracharya was devoted to the worship of Shiva.

Advaita Vedanta Monasteries

Adi Shankaracharya had established four monasteries or *Mathas* in the four corners of India and they are still standing there today providing guiding leadership to the Advaita community:

1. Sarada Matha in Sringeri in the South
2. Kalika Matha in Dvaraka in the West
3. Jyoti Matha in Badari in the North
4. Govardhan Matha in Puri in the East

The following organizations also support Advaita Vedanta:

- Ramakrishna Mission, headquartered in Kolkata, has centers all over India in the metropolitan and second-tier cities. They have also overseas centers in all major cities of the world. Swami Vivekananda, a disciple of Ramakrishna, was the force behind this mission that has existed for more than a hundred years.
- Chinmaya Mission has centers all over India and abroad. Swami Chinmayananda, a disciple of Swami Sivananda was the spirit behind the mission.
- Sivananda Ashram in Rishikesh is the headquarters of the Divine Life Society which has centers all over the world.

Swami Sivananda was the force behind it.

Advaita Sangha

Wherever there is a center for Advaita Vedanta, a community of practitioners is developed. Each of these centers is supported by the Advaita organizations by providing trained teachers and Swamis to lead the respective communities.

7.2.2 Advaita Scriptures

The main Upanishads, Brahma Sutras, and Bhagavad Gita are considered the main scriptures for Vedanta. The commentaries written by Adi Shankaracharya on the above three texts are considered principal scriptures for Advaita Vedanta. Other books of importance to Advaita are listed below:

1. Tatwabodha by Adi Shankaracharya
2. Vivekachudamani by Adi Shankaracharya
3. Atmabodha by Adi Shankaracharya
4. Brahma-siddhi by Mandana Mishra
5. Mandukya Upanishad, commentary by Goudapada
6. Pancadasi by Vidyaranya

The following books published in the more recent times are of interest to Advaita.

1. Astavakra Samhita
2. Advaita Sidhi by Madhusudan Saraswati, 1917

We give a summary of a few of the important scriptures.

Brahma Sutra also known as Vedanta Sutra, is attributed to Badarayana and Vyasa and composed between 500 BCE and 200 BCE. It summarizes the main findings from the Upanishads.

- Brahman is the ultimate reality and the world comes into existence through

    Brahman. It quotes Taittriya, Chandogya,

    Kaushitaki, Mundaka, Katha,

Brihadaranyaka, and Prashna Upanishads to prove that Brahman is the efficient and material cause of the world. That the Brahman and the empirical world are one. That *Avidya* is the root cause of evil.

- Bhramasutra Bhasya by Adi Shankaracharya is a commentary and is a pivotal text for Advaita Vedanta [36].

   Gaudapada Karika is a commentary on Manduka Upanishad by Gaudapada, the teacher's teacher of Adi Shankaracharya. The self remains in one's body in three states: the waking state when he experiences the world, the dreaming state when he experiences mind objects *Taijasa*, and the deep sleep state when he experiences *Prajna*. There is a fourth state *Turiya*, which is a non-dual state and that is *Atman* [37].

   Bhagavad Gita is the most sacred scripture in Sanatana Dharma. It describes the godhead Krishana instructing his friend Arjuna at the battlefield of Kurukshetra. Arjuna is dejected to wage battle against the Kauravas and their supporters as the Kauravas were their cousin brothers. Krishna talks about the world, the eternal soul or *Atman* in every individual. That one has to do his duty, even if it means killing one's own kins if it is to uphold the *Dharma*. Gita explains the path of Karma Yoga and *Jnana* Yoga and is an indispensable scripture to guide the lives of all [38, 39].

   Pancadasi of Sri Vidyaranya Swami, Head of Sringeri Matha from 1377 CE to 1386 CE, is an Advaita Vedanta manual for the followers of Advaita. The text is divided into five chapters each on Discrimination, Consciousness and Bliss, thus corresponding to the three aspects of Brahman: *Sat*, *Cit* and *Ananda* [40].

7.2.3 Advaita Liturgy

In this section, we focus on the liturgical aspects of practicing Advaita Vedanta and specifically examine the following aspects of the practice:

1. Prayers, Songs and Mantras

2. Vows and Precepts

3. Statues and Images

Prayers, Songs and Mantras

There are hundreds of prayers, songs, and mantras in use by the Vedantic community and here we give just a few examples.

Bhaja Govindam Stotra by Adi Shankaracharya [41]:

• Bhaja Govindam, Bhaja Govindam

Govindam Bhaja MoodhaMate,

Sampratte Sannihitke Kale

Nahi Nahi Rakshati Dookrunj Karane...

Dashasloki Stotra is the version defining the self by Adi Shankaracharya and given below is the first verse and the meaning [42].

• Na bhuumirna toyam na tejo na vaayuh

Na kham nendriyam vaa na teshham

Samuuhah

Anekaantikatvaat.h sushnuptyekasiddah

Tadeko.avashishhtah shivah kevalo.aham.h

Meaning:

I am not the earth or water or fire or air or space. Neither am I any of the faculties or their aggregate. I am not these as they are all uncertain. I am proved in the experience of deep sleep, the auspicious residue only am I.

Hari-meede Stotra is another very popular song in the praise of Hari or Vishnu, composed by Adi Shankaracharya [43].

Ahamgraha Upasana is a mantra for Vedantic meditation [44].

- Om

  Aham Brahma Asmi

  Soham

  Sivoham

  Satchidananda Svarupoham

Advaita Vows and Precepts

Though belief and practice in Advaita Vedanta do not require you to take specific views, the seekers looking for the ultimate realization are strongly encouraged to take the '*Sannyasa*' from worldly affairs. All the great Advaita masters reaching that supreme liberation had taken *Sannyasa* vows in the formative years of their journey:

- Adi Shankaracharya
- Vivekananda
- Ramana Maharshi

There have been great learned men, kings, merchants and even Rishis, who had lived as householders entangled with the world, but they had to ultimately become *Sannyasins* to pursue the ultimate:

- Yajnavalkya
- King Janaka

Sanatana Dharma provides the four *Varnashrama* stages to provide an escape route to the seekers at any of the first three stages: *Brahmacharya, Grihastha, Vanaprastha,* and *Sannyasa*.

What is utmost required for the seeker is to live a disciplined life controlling the senses and lead a virtuous life [45]. All the basic requirements of Yoga are a good outline to guide the life of the seekers to ultimately yoke with the ultimate [46].

Adi Shankaracharya had exhorted that one has to undergo the disciplinary stages of *Viveka, Vairagya, Sama, Dama, Uparati, Titiksha, Sraddha, Samadhana,* and *Mumukshutva* [47]. One has to be well developed in all these qualities to travel in the ultimate path.

Advaita Statues and Images

Ishvara is the reflection of the ultimate reality in Advaita Vedanta and the practitioner can worship any of the godheads generally prevalent in Sanatana Dharma depending upon their individual preferences from any of the gods and goddesses. Shiva, Vishnu, and Shakti are the main three types of deities revered in Vedanta.

- Shiva is worshipped in the form of Nataraja, or a Lingam, or as Mt. Kailash, or without any symbol. Shiva represents 'The Destroyer' aspect of Brahman. One can simply chant 'Om Namah Shivaya'. The song of a follower of Vedanta is: 'Shivoham Shivoham Shivoham Soham Sachidananda- Svarupoham' [48].

- Vishnu is 'The One who Pervades' aspect of Brahman and is also known as Hari and Narayana. Vishnu descends in the world as an Avatar (reincarnation) to restore cosmic order and protect Dharma. Rama and Krishna are the main Avatars of Vishnu.

- Shakti is regarded as the feminine power running the universe. As a goddess, she is the consort of Shiva. Similarly, Lakshmi is considered the consort of Vishnu.

7.2.4 Advaita Stories and Enquiries

There is a strong tradition of conveying the ultimate truth through stories and inquiries in the Vedas and the Upanishads. In that sense, they are similar to the Koans used in Zen Buddhism. Some specific stories and inquiries that should be noted here are the following:

1. The story of Nachiketa's request to Yama [49]
2. The story of Maitreyee's asking Yajnavalkya [50]
3. The Enquiry 'Who am I?' [51]

7.2.5 Meditation

As per Swami Sivananda, 'meditation starts with duality and ends in the glorious consciousness of the unity of life' [52]. The meditator, the aspirant towards liberation and ultimate connection with the transcendental power of the universe must be ready and willing to persevere in the path.

Certain environments make meditation more powerful. For example, vast open areas in the mountains or near the water bodies produce special energy during meditations. One usually faces the north or the east during the meditation. Midnight to 4 AM is considered the best time suited for deep meditation [53].

One sits on a special mat made of soft natural material rather than the ground to avoid shorting the electrical energy generated to the ground. The spinal cord has to be erect to facilitate easy breathing. You can meditate on the Brahman by experiencing its reflection in the self, the *Atman*. One can attend the *Turiya* or the fourth state, the non-dual state of deep bliss [54].

7.3 Comparative Analysis

Both Zen Buddhism and Advaita Vedanta started around the same time between the sixth and eighth century CE and have a history of more than a thousand years of continuous development and practice. As a result, Zen institutions have developed extensively in Japan, Korea, Vietnam, and China. In the twentieth and twenty first century, Zen has spread to Europe and the Americas. Similarly, Advaita Vedanta spread widely over India during the last thousand years. There was more of a renewal and reinvigoration of Advaita Vedanta in the 19th and 20th centuries in India due to the emergence of new movements as a reaction to the domination by the colonial powers in India.

Practice in Zen Buddhism is very much evident in the more than fifteen thousand Zen temples in Japan and more intensively in the dozens of large Zen monasteries in Japan. One can see the practice of Advaita Vedanta in the large number of *Mathas* established by the Advaita organizations. However, the practice is not explicitly present in the thousands of temples in India, since the temples are not segregated as such by their practice of philosophy, but rather by the *Ishvara* that is enshrined there. The Zen monasteries in Japan have temporal and administrative authority over the Zen temples operating there. There is no such control authority in India over the myriads of temples, the *Mathas* only show the directions and offer special teaching services as requested.

As far as scriptures are concerned, most of the important sutras used in Zen practice were originally written in Sanskrit and translated versions are available in Chinese, Japanese, Korean, Tibetan, English, and other languages. There is also a vast array of Mahayana texts known as *Shastras* which are available in Sanskrit and other languages. The Japanese use a Japanized version of Sanskrit during Zen practice in Zen. In the United States, a mixture of English and Japanese versions of the sutras are used depending upon the choice of the particular monastery.

Advaita Vedanta has an extensive literature, written mostly in Sanskrit. Most of them are also available now in translated form in English. Selected few of them are available in Indian vernacular languages too.

Liturgical practices in Zen and Advaita Vedanta are different. Zen has a more formalized and explicit set of rules and procedures.

Just as Koans are used in Zen as a device to advance the practitioner in the path of enlightenment, special stories and inquiries are experienced in Advaita Vedanta to aid in the path of liberation.

Finally, the goals of meditation in both the practices are the same, enlightenment or liberation. The meditation procedures and practices are similar, but Zen organizations have lot more formal avenues for meditation practice through regular retreats organized on a monthly, quarterly, and annual basis.

References

1. *Zen Enlightenment: Origin and Meaning, H. Dumolin, Shambala Press, 1979, Page 77*

2. *Zen Buddhism: Doctrinal Foundations and Practice, V. Panigrahi, A K Mishra Publishers, 2021, Page 79-83*

3. *Perfection of Wisdom: The Short Prajnaparamita Texts, Edward Conze, Buddhist Publishing Group, 2002*

4. Buddhist Scriptures, Edward Conze, Penguin, 1959
5. The Heart Sutra, Bill Porter, Counterpoint, 2005
6. Zen Buddhism: Doctrinal Foundations and Practice, Varish Panigrahi, A K Mishra Publishers, 2021, Page 58-67
7. The Vajrachhedika in Buddhist Mahayana Texts, F. MaxMuller, Motilal Banarasidass, 2005
8. Buddhist Wisdom: The Diamond Sutra and the Heart Sutra, Edward Conze, Random House, 2001
9. Zen Buddhism: Doctrinal Foundations and Practice, V. Panigrahi, A K Mishra Publishers, 2021, Page 67-71
10. The Lotus Sutra, Burton Watson, Columbia University Press, 1994
11. The Lotus Sutra: A Contemporary Translation of a Buddhist Classic, Gene Reeves, Wisdom Publications, 2008
12. Zen Buddhism: Doctrinal Foundations and Practice, V. Panigrahi, A K Mishra Publishers, 2021, Page 71-74
13. The Lankavatara Sutra: A Mahayana Text, D.T Suzuki, Munshiram Manoharlal, 2013
14. The Heart Sutra, Bill Porter, Counterpoint, 2013
15. Zen Buddhism: Doctrinal Foundations and Practice, Varish Panigrahi, A K Mishra Publishers, 2021, Page 74-77
16. The Flower Ornament Scripture: A Translation of the Avatamsaka Sutra, Thomas Cleary, 1993
17. Mahayana Buddhism: The Doctrinal Foundations, Paul Williams

18. *The Vimalakirti Sutra*, Burton Watson, Columbia University Press, 1997

19. *The Holy Teaching of Vimalakirti: A Mahayana Scripture*, Robert Thurman, Pennsylvania State University Press, 2000

20. *Buddhist Bible*, Dwight Goddard, Beacon Press, 1938

21. *'Arriving Home'* Website, Richard Jones

22. *Manual of Zen Buddhism*, D.T Suzuki, Grove Weidenfeld, 1960, Page 151-152

23. Ibid Page 89-103

24. *Zen Buddhism: Doctrinal Foundations and Practice*, Varish Panigrahi, A K Mishra Publishers, 2021, Page 95

25. *Manual of Zen Buddhism*, D.T Suzuki, Grove Weidenfeld, 1960, Page 163-167

26. *Meeting the Buddha: A Guide to Buddhas, Bodhisattvas and Tantric Deities*, Vassantara, Motilal Banarasidass, 2007

27. *Zen Flesh and Zen Bones*, Paul Reps and Nyogen Senzaki, Tuttle Publishing, 1985, Page 109-162

28. *The Blue Cliff Records: The Hekiga New tab n Roku*, R.D.M Shaw, Michae Joseph, London, 1961

29. *The Blue Cliff Record*, Thomas Cleary and J.C Cleary, Shambala Publications, 2005

30. *Book of Serenity: One Hundred Zen Dialogues*, Thomas Cleary, Shambala Publications, Boston, 1988

31. Master Dogen's Shinzi Shobogenzo : 301 Koan Stories, Godo Nishijima, Windbell Publication, 2003

32. *On Zen Practice: Body, Breathe and Mind*, Taizan Maezumi and Bernie Glarman, Wisdom Publications, 2002

33. *Morning Dewdrops of the Mind: Teachings of a Contemporary Zen Master*, Shodo Harada, Nath Atlantic Books, 1993, Page 69

34. *Zen Meditation in Plain English*, John Daishin Buksbazen, Wisden Publications, 2002

35. *The Rinzai Zen Way: A Guide to Practice*, Meido Moore, Shambhala Publications, 2018

36. *Brahma Sutra Bhasya of Shankaracharya*, Swami Gambhirananda, Advaita Ashrama Publications, 1991

37. *Gaudapada Karika*, R.D. Karmarkar, Bhandarkar Oriental Research Institute, 1953

38. *Shrimad Bhagavat Gita : Sadhaka Sanjivani*, Gita Press, Gorakhpur, 1997

39. *The Bhagavat Gita*, Eknath Eshwram and Daina Morrison, Penguin Books, Delhi, 1986

40. *Pancadasi of Sri Vidyaranya Swami*, Swami Swahananda, Sri Ramakrishna Math, 1967

41. *Bhaja Govindam Stotra*, Adi Shankaracharya

42. *Dashasloki Stotra*, Adi Shankaracharya

43. *Hari- Meede Stotra*, Adi Shankaracharya

44. *Essence of Vedanta*, Swami Sivananda, The Divine Life Society, 1989, Page 231

45. Ibid Page 280-283

46. *An Introduction to Indian Philosophy*, Satischandra Chatterjee and Dhirendraohan Datta, Rupa Publications, New Delhi, 2007, Page 271

47. *Essence of Vedanta*, Swami Sivananda, The Divine Life Society, 1989, Page 97

48. *Ibid Page 230*

49. *Discourse on Katho Upanishad, Swami Chinmayanand, Chinmaya Publishers, Madras*

50. *Brihadaranyaka Upanishad*

51. *The Collected Works of Ramana Maharshi, Arthur Osborne, Page 39*

52. *Essence of Vedanta, Swami Sivananda, The Divine Life Society, 1989, Page 99*

53. *Ibid Page 101*

54. *Ibid Page 109*

Chapter 8

Concluding Remarks

The comparative analysis of Zen Buddhism and Advaita Vedanta showcases two distinct yet fascinating approaches to understanding the nature of reality by achieving spiritual enlightenment. Further, both traditions offer valuable insights into the human quest for transcending the confines of ordinary dualistic or conditioned thinking and experiencing a much deeper, insightful, and profound understanding of reality. Both traditions have distinctly evolved, Advaita Vedanta exclusively in India and Zen in China and Japan, revealing a rich tapestry of philosophical, spiritual, and practical traditions and sharing deep historical roots in Indian, Chinese, and Japanese civilizations.

Zen Buddhism is poised as an interpretation of the Buddha's message, based on the Mahayana school of understanding, whereas Advaita Vedanta is the most comprehensive school of non-duality in Hinduism based on an interpretation of the Upanishads and the Brahma Sutras. A comparative study such as this highlights the diversity within Eastern philosophy through these two traditions. Both traditions are distinct schools of thought that approach fundamental questions about the nature of reality, and the spiritual awakening to understand it by transcending the self.

The most observable difference between Zen Buddhism and Advaita Vedanta is that the former emphasizes the 'direct experience' and 'mindfulness' as means to achieve spiritual enlightenment. The latter relies on the realization of a non-dual consciousness called Brahman through self-inquiry and scriptural study. But the overall process employed by both traditions is to find a way to reach the goal of transcending the limitations of dualistic or conditioned thinking and complete the quest for ultimate truth and enlightenment. Zen Buddhism rooted in Mahayana Buddhist tradition, hypothesizes the doctrine of emptiness (*Sunyata*), which is the theory that all phenomena are devoid of any inherent, and fixed existence. Their existence is momentary (*Kshanika*), their state is transient and their effect is impermanent. Besides, the concept of Buddha-nature is paramount in Zen. It is the understanding that every sentient being possesses an innate, and enlightened nature that can be realized through practicing Zazen and mindfulness.

On the other hand, Advaita Vedanta is a non-dualistic school of Hindu philosophy that asserts the oneness or unity of the ultimate reality (*Brahman*) and individual soul (*Atman*). It proposes an elaborate exploration of metaphysics, asserting the multiplicity of the world, and calling it an illusion (*Maya*). The concept of *Maya* is central to Advaita Vedanta which explains the nature of an illusionary reality and how this reality is perceived because of *Avidya* or ignorance. But beneath this illusion, there is a unity and non-conditionality called *Brahman*. The methodology employed in Advaita Vedanta is contemplation on abstract metaphysical concepts and rigorous study of scriptures, to understand the unity of the self and ultimate reality called *Brahman*.

The comparative analysis of epistemology in both traditions sheds light on the nuanced ways through which both approach the acquisition of knowledge and the understanding of such knowledge. Zen Buddhism believes that a direct understanding of reality is based on intuition and is achieved through mindfulness and meditation. The importance of scriptural authority is limited to being helpful in the process of understanding and not in the achievement of enlightenment. Scriptures (sutras) are often viewed as useful guides and references, but not as the exclusive source of wisdom. In this regard, Zen Buddhism has a more flexible approach to scriptural authority compared to other Buddhist traditions. Besides placing its primary focus on the immediate or direct experience as a means of understanding reality and attaining enlightenment, Zen also promotes its reliance on Zazen (sitting meditation) and mindfulness to gain insight. Often employed in Zen are the techniques of paradoxical questioning through Koans to challenge the limitations of conventional or ordinary thinking. It emphasizes intuitive understanding over rational analysis. Zen also stresses the limitations of vernacular expressions and often highlights the understanding gained through 'transmission beyond words and letters'. It is an important aspect of Zen which states that ultimate understanding cannot be comprehended through language or explanation and must necessarily be realized through personal experience.

On the other hand, Advaita Vedanta places a strong emphasis on scriptural authority. Sacred scriptures like the Upanishads and Brahma Sutras are essential sources of knowledge and guides to philosophical inquiry in Advaita Vedanta. Besides a key technique employed in Advaita epistemology is self-inquiry or *Atma-Vichara*. This involves rigorous introspection into the metaphysical claims of the above scriptures by questioning the identity of the self. Concepts and metaphysical principles play a central role in Advaita epistemology. It encourages philosophical inquiry and promotes intellectual understanding of the non-dual nature of reality.

Zen Buddhism is uniquely positioned among other Buddhist traditions, in the sense that it is less concerned with moral codes and settings and more focused on the ethical dimension of being fully present in one's actions, by practicing mindfulness and awareness of the present moment. However, ethics is not entirely neglected by Zen as it is often characterized by a commitment to minimalism in lifestyle, simplicity in action, compassion, and nonattachment. The practice of non-attachment to actions is a central Buddhist teaching followed profoundly in Zen because it encourages a practitioner to let go of his desires, which are the root cause of all sufferings. It also highlights the mindset of a Bodhisattva and proposes that appropriate ethical conduct naturally arises from the mind of a person who has awakened and is aware of the present, or is enlightened. Hence, ethical behavior is not dictated by rules but rather is a product of one's awareness. The question of what is the right action is answered by Zen by highlighting the importance of implementing complete awareness and undivided attention in each act and performing it out of compassion and non-attachment. This promotes harmony within oneself and with others.

Advaita Vedanta however, acknowledges the importance of moral conduct (*Dharma*) as a primary step in one's spiritual pursuit. Ethical principles are considered essential for purifying the mind and body, thus creating a conducive environment for self-realization. Virtues like truthfulness, nonviolence, and self-discipline are prerequisites for effective practice. Actions are strongly believed to have consequences according to Advaita and hence the adherence to the law of karma and the justification for cause and effect is integral to Advaita Vedanta's ethical structure. Overall, it considers purifying the mind as a preparatory but necessary phase for a practitioner to align his life to the demands of self-realization.

The aesthetics of Zen Buddhism and Advaita Vedanta share certain common elements but mostly exhibit a distinct but reflective understanding based on the unique philosophical foundations they are based on. Zen believes in seeing the beauty in the everyday mundane objects of the natural and man-made world, including the things that are irregular, asymmetrical, and antique. It embodies the principles of Wabi-Sabi which is the valued appreciation for things that are imperfect, impermanent, and simple. It also promotes appreciation of art and design through minimalistic expression, characterized by simple designs. The idea employed in Zen is to employ simplicity in one's actions and activities which supposedly helps one find clarity and focus in life. Zen also encourages one to achieve awareness of the present moment and see the beauty in it, i.e. what is happening right now is beautiful. Zen actively draws inspiration from the natural world, incorporating elements like water, plants, and rocks in their artworks. It highlights the interconnectedness of the phenomenal world through its integration with the natural world.

In Advaita Vedanta, aesthetics is an emphasis on the eternal and sublime aspects of existence that are reflected in the portrayal of diverse images and deities, intriguing art and architecture, and elaborate rituals, most of which are awe-inspiring and grandiose. The designs in the artwork are highly symbolic and meaningful. Besides, the designs are often a detailed or elaborative display of ideas, beliefs, and philosophy. The art is also known for its use of colors and intricate patterns. The idea is to have a glimpse of the divine through art which is the vibrant source of all life. Often exaggerated and elaborative use of rituals are employed to evoke the ever presence of the divine. From the above, it can be concluded that while Zen emphasizes on the simplicity and the beauty of imperfection, Advaita embraces the grandiose, vibrant, and symbolic expression of the divine expressed through the arts.

A Zen practitioner aims to develop mindfulness in each situation and to achieve awareness even in the most menial activity. For this, the practice of meditation is primarily employed in Zen. Practices like Zazen (sitting meditation), Kinhin (waking meditation), Dokusan (personal discussion with the master), tea ceremony (ChanoyU), and rigorous Koan studies are employed in Zen.

On the other hand, the key practice in Advaita Vedanta is the employment of self-inquiry (*Atma Vichara*). It is a self-investigative practice to unveil the true nature of the self (*Atman*) and inquire into its source and destination. Besides the practice of studying sacred texts like the Upanishads, the Brahma Sutras and the Bhagavad Gita is nonnegotiable in Advaita Vedanta. Advaita practitioners read a great deal about the works of Adi Shankaracharya and other Advaita masters that provide philosophical foundations for self-inquiry. Besides, devotional practices like *Japa*, or the repetitive recitation of important mantras or the name of any deity are common in Advaita. Satsang associations are also regularly practiced which are seen as a means to purify the mind and cultivate devotion besides *Japa* and *Mantra* recitations. Unlike Zen, in Advaita Vedanta, meditation is not a prominent aspect of practice. It is practiced in a personal capacity. It can vary in form and content, like guided meditations, or breathing control, or contemplation of specific concepts.

Zen Buddhism and Advaita Vedanta, are unique non-dual philosophies, that give due importance to the direct experience of the true nature of reality. Zen employs meditation and Koans as practical tools in its methods, but Advaita Vedanta relies on the intellectual inquiry leading up to selfrealization. This book offers a comprehensive report on the similarities and differences between Zen Buddhism and Advaita Vedanta. In the scope of further study, investigating the effect of these philosophies as applied and practiced in the modern context would be useful. Since both traditions have evolved for over a thousand years with an unbroken chain of transmission of knowledge from the teacher to the student, both traditions can be credited with having influenced and touched the lives of scores of people. There is potential for interfaith dialogues and spiritual syncretism between Zen and Advaita Vedanta.

Black Eagle Books

www.blackeaglebooks.org
info@blackeaglebooks.org

Black Eagle Books, an independent publisher, was founded as a nonprofit organization in April, 2019. It is our mission to connect and engage the Indian diaspora and the world at large with the best of works of world literature published on a collaborative platform, with special emphasis on foregrounding Contemporary Classics and New Writing.

www.ingramcontent.com/pod-product-compliance
Lightning Source LLC
Chambersburg PA
CBHW060558080526
44585CB00013B/606